Parties & Potlucks

Publications International, Ltd.

Photography on pages 42, 51, 52, 60, 62, 70, 71, 72, 95, 139, 155, 162, 167, 168, 177, 180, 201, 207, 220, 227, 228, 229, 231, 232, 234, 236, 240, 241 and 243 by PIL Photo Studio.
Photographer: Justin Paris
Photographer's Assistant: Sandy Rosencrans
Food Stylists: Kim Hartman, Kathy Joy, Mary Ann Melone, Josephine Orba
Food Stylists' Assistants: Brittany Culver, Elaine Funk, Lissa Levy

Pictured on the front cover (from top): Chocolate Orange Fondue *(page 237)* and Best Asian-Style Ribs *(page 24)*.
Pictured on the back cover (clockwise from top): Feta and Mint Spread *(page 226)*, Brats in Beer *(page 16)*, Spanish Paella-Style Rice *(page 162)* and Pancetta Horseradish Dip *(page 229)*.

ISBN-13: 978-1-4508-3354-7
ISBN-10: 1-4508-3354-3

Library of Congress Control Number: 2011932206

Manufactured in China.

8 7 6 5 4 3 2 1

Table of Contents

Slow Cooking Hints and Tips

How to get the best results from your CROCK-POT® slow cooker

Your **CROCK-POT®** slow cooker can be the best kitchen assistant you've ever had. Your family will enjoy delicious meals, and you'll save time and effort, thanks to the flavorful cooking process that works while you're away from home.

Your **CROCK-POT®** slow cooker can also help you entertain guests. It makes a great server for hot beverages, appetizers, or dips. Just keep it on the WARM setting to maintain the proper serving temperature.

To get the most from your **CROCK-POT®** slow cooker, keep the following hints and tips in mind.

Adding Ingredients at the End of the Cooking Time

Certain ingredients are best added toward the end of the cooking time. These include:

- **Milk, sour cream, and yogurt:** Add during the last 15 minutes.
- **Seafood and fish:** Add during the last 15 to 30 minutes.
- **Fresh herbs:** Fresh herbs such as basil will darken with long cooking, so if you want colorful fresh herbs, add them during the last 15 minutes of cooking or directly to the dish just before serving it.

Pasta and Rice

For slow-cooked rice dishes, converted rice holds up best through longer cooking times. Most recipes suggest adding pasta or rice halfway through the cooking time for the best texture. If the rice doesn't seem completely cooked after the suggested time, add an extra ½ cup to 1 cup of liquid per cup of rice, and extend the cooking time by 30 to 60 minutes.

Cooking Temperatures and Food Safety

According to the U.S. Department of Agriculture, bacteria in food is killed at a temperature of 165°F. As a result, it's important to follow the recommended cooking times and to keep the cover on your **CROCK-POT®** slow cooker during the cooking process to maintain food-safe temperatures. Slow-cooked meats and poultry are best when simmered gently for the period of time that allows the connective tissues to break down, yielding meat that is fall-off-the-bone tender and juicy.

If your food isn't done after 8 hours when the recipe calls for cooking 8 to 10 hours, this could be due to altitude, extreme humidity, or voltage variations, which are commonplace. Slight

Slow Cooking Hints and Tips

fluctuations in power do not have a noticeable effect on most appliances; however, they can slightly alter the cooking times. Always allow your food to continue cooking until it's done.

If you arrive home and find the electrical power service to your home is out, check the **CROCK-POT®** slow cooker immediately. Check the temperature of the contents in the **CROCK-POT®** slow cooker with an instant-read thermometer. If the temperature is above 140°F, you can transfer the contents to a large saucepan or Dutch oven and finish cooking it on a gas range or gas grill. However, if the temperature of the contents is between 40° and 140°F, you should throw the food away.

If the electricity is on when you arrive home, but you can tell by the clocks that your home has been without power, the best thing to do is throw away the food. You'll never know what the temperature of the food was when the power went off or how long it was off; the food may have spent several hours in the danger zone. And, although the food is hot when you get home and looks done, it's better to err on the side of safety and throw it away.

Allow plenty of time for cooking. Remember, it's practically impossible to overcook food in a **CROCK-POT®** slow cooker. You'll learn through experience whether to decrease or increase cooking times for your recipes.

Browning Meat

Meat will not brown as it would if it were cooked in a skillet or oven at a high temperature. It's not necessary to brown meat before slow cooking. However, if you prefer the look and flavor of browned meat, just brown it in a large skillet coated with oil, butter, or nonstick cooking spray, then place the browned ingredients into the stoneware and follow the recipe as written.

Herbs and Spices

When cooking with your **CROCK-POT®** slow cooker, use dried and ground herbs and spices, which work well during long cook times. However, the flavor and aroma of crushed or ground herbs may differ depending on their shelf life, and their flavor can lessen during the extended cooking time in the **CROCK-POT®** slow cooker. Be sure to taste the finished dish and add more seasonings if needed. If you prefer colorful fresh herbs, add them during the last 15 minutes of cooking time or to the dish as a garnish. Fresh herbs add both color and flavor to most dishes.

Cooking for Larger Quantity Yields

If you want to make a bigger batch in a larger unit, such as a 5-, 6-, or 7-quart **CROCK-POT®** slow cooker, guidelines for doubling or tripling ingredients include:

- When preparing dishes with beef or pork in a larger unit, browning the meat in a skillet before adding it to the **CROCK-POT®** slow cooker yields the best results; the meat will cook more evenly.
- Roasted meats, chicken, and turkey quantities may be doubled or tripled, and seasonings adjusted by half. Caution: Flavorful dried spices such as garlic or chili powder will intensify during long, slow cooking. Add just 25 to 50 percent more spices, as needed, to balance the flavors.
- When preparing a soup or a stew, you may double all ingredients except the liquids, seasonings, and dried herbs. Increase liquid volume by half, or adjust as needed. The **CROCK-POT®** slow cooker lid collects steam, which condenses to keep foods moist and to maintain liquid volume.
- To avoid over or undercooking, always fill the stoneware 1/2 to 3/4 full and conform to the recommended cook times (unless instructed otherwise by our slow cooker recipes).

Slow Cooking Hints and Tips

• Do not double thickeners, such as cornstarch, at the beginning. You may always add more thickener later if it's necessary.

Cooking with Frozen Foods

You may cook frozen foods in your **CROCK-POT®** slow cooker. For best results, use the following guidelines:

• Add at least 1 cup of warm or hot liquid to the stoneware before placing frozen meat in the **CROCK-POT®** slow cooker.

• Do not preheat the **CROCK-POT®** slow cooker.

• Cook recipes containing frozen meats for an additional 4 to 6 hours on LOW or 2 hours on HIGH.

• Slow cooking frozen foods requires a longer cook time than fresh foods because the food needs more time to come up to safe internal temperatures. Meats also will require additional time to allow them to become tender. If there is any question about the cooking time, use a thermometer to ensure meats are cooking appropriately.

High-Altitude Adjustments

If you live at an altitude above 3,500 feet, you'll need to make some adjustments when slow cooking. Everything will take longer to cook, so plan for that. Tough meats take longer to become tender at high altitudes—sometimes much longer. Try cooking on the HIGH heat setting instead of LOW. Root vegetables also take longer to cook; for quicker cooking, cut them into smaller pieces than the recipe suggests.

Removable Stoneware

The removable stoneware in your **CROCK-POT®** slow cooker makes cleaning easy. However, the stoneware insert can be damaged by sudden

changes in temperature. Here are tips on the use and care of your stoneware:

• Many stoneware cooking inserts are safe for use in a conventional or microwave oven.

• Because all **CROCK-POT®** slow cookers have wrap-around heat, there's no direct heat at the bottom. Always fill the stoneware at least half full to conform to recommended times for best results. Smaller quantities can still be cooked, but cooking times will be affected.

• Don't preheat the **CROCK-POT®** slow cooker. Don't place a cold insert into a preheated base.

• Don't place a hot insert on a cold surface or in the refrigerator; don't fill it with cold water.

• Never place stoneware in the freezer.

• If you place ingredients in the stoneware and refrigerate the stoneware overnight, additional cooking time will be required to cook the food safely and appropriately. If there is any question about the cooking time, use a thermometer to ensure meats have cooked appropriately.

• Don't use the stoneware insert if it's cracked; replace it.

• For further safety tips, please refer to the instruction manual that came with your **CROCK-POT®** slow cooker.

Tailgating

Bacon-Wrapped Fingerling Potatoes with Thyme

1 pound fingerling potatoes
2 tablespoons olive oil
1 tablespoon minced fresh thyme
1/2 teaspoon black pepper
1/4 teaspoon paprika
1/2 pound bacon
1/4 cup chicken broth

1. Toss potatoes with oil, thyme, pepper and paprika in large bowl.

2. Cut each bacon slice in half lengthwise; wrap half slice bacon tightly around each potato.

3. Heat large skillet over medium heat; add potatoes. Reduce heat to medium-low; cook until lightly browned and bacon has tightened around potatoes.

4. Place potatoes in **CROCK-POT®** slow cooker. Add broth. Cover; cook on HIGH 3 hours.

Makes 4 to 6 servings

Tip: This appetizer can be made even more eye-catching with rare varieties of potatoes. Many interesting types of small potatoes can be found at farmers' markets. Purple potatoes, about the size of fingerling potatoes, can add some more color and spunk to this dish.

Meatball Grinders

- **1 can (about 14 ounces) diced tomatoes, drained and juices reserved**
- **1 can (8 ounces) no-salt-added tomato sauce**
- **1/4 cup chopped onion**
- **2 tablespoons tomato paste**
- **1 teaspoon Italian seasoning**
- **1 pound ground chicken**
- **1/2 cup fresh whole wheat or white bread crumbs (1 slice bread)**
- **1 egg white, lightly beaten**
- **3 tablespoons finely chopped fresh parsley**
- **2 cloves garlic, minced**
- **1/4 teaspoon salt**
- **1/8 teaspoon black pepper**
- **4 small hard rolls, split**
- **2 tablespoons grated Parmesan cheese**

1. Combine diced tomatoes, 1/2 cup reserved juice, tomato sauce, onion, tomato paste and Italian seasoning in **CROCK-POT®** slow cooker. Cover; cook on LOW 3 to 4 hours.

2. Prepare meatballs halfway through cooking time. Combine chicken, bread crumbs, egg white, parsley, garlic, salt and pepper in medium bowl. With wet hands, form mixture into 12 to 16 meatballs. Coat medium nonstick skillet with cooking spray; heat over medium heat. Add meatballs; cook 8 to 10 minutes or until well browned on all sides. Transfer meatballs to **CROCK-POT®** slow cooker. Cover; cook on LOW 1 to 2 hours or until meatballs are no longer pink in centers and are heated through.

3. Place 3 to 4 meatballs in each roll. Spoon sauce over meatballs. Sprinkle with cheese.

Makes 4 servings

Chunky Veggie Dip

- 1 red bell pepper, chopped
- 1 green bell pepper, chopped
- 1/2 onion, finely chopped
- 1 stalk celery, chopped
- 2 tablespoons water
- 1/8 teaspoon red pepper flakes
- 1/4 cup milk
- 3/4 teaspoon cornstarch
- 1 cup (4 ounces) shredded sharp Cheddar cheese
- 2 ounces cream cheese
- 1 jar (4 ounces) diced pimiento
- 3/4 teaspoon salt
- Baked corn tortilla chips

1. Coat **CROCK-POT®** slow cooker with nonstick cooking spray. Add bell peppers, onion, celery, water and red pepper flakes. Cover; cook on LOW 3 hours or until celery is tender.

2. Combine milk and cornstarch in small bowl, stirring until cornstarch dissolves. Add to pepper mixture with Cheddar and cream cheese. Press down on cream cheese with rubber spatula until well blended. Stir in pimiento and salt. Cover; cook 15 minutes or until thickened. Serve with tortilla chips.

Makes 12 servings

Variation: Use soft corn tortillas instead of chips. Cut each tortilla into 6 wedges and bake in a single layer on a baking sheet at 350°F for 10 minutes. Cool completely before serving. Chips will firm as they cool.

Tropical Chicken Wings

- 1 jar (12 ounces) pineapple preserves
- 1/2 cup soy sauce
- 1/2 cup chopped green onions
- 3 tablespoons fresh lime juice
- 2 tablespoons pomegranate molasses or honey (see Tip)
- 1 tablespoon minced garlic
- 2 teaspoons sriracha sauce*
- 1/4 teaspoon ground allspice
- 3 pounds chicken wings, tips removed and split at the joint
- 1 tablespoon toasted sesame seeds

****Sriracha is a spicy chile sauce made from dried chiles and used as a condiment in several Asian cuisines. It can be found in the ethnic section of major supermarkets, but an equal amount of hot pepper sauce may be substituted.***

1. Combine all ingredients except chicken wings and sesame seeds in **CROCK-POT®** slow cooker; stir well.

2. Add chicken wings to sauce and stir to coat. Cover; cook on LOW 3 to 4 hours or until wings are fork-tender.

3. Sprinkle with sesame seeds just before serving.

Makes 6 to 8 servings

Tip: Pomegranate molasses is a syrup made from pomegranate juice cooked with sugar. You can easily make your own if it isn't in the ethnic foods aisle of your local supermarket. For this recipe, bring to a boil 1/2 cup pomegranate juice, 2 tablespoons sugar and 1 teaspoon lemon juice in a small saucepan over medium-high heat. Cook, stirring occasionally, until reduced to about 2 tablespoons. Use as directed above.

Brats in Beer

- $1^1/_2$ **pounds bratwurst (about 5 or 6 links)**
- 1 **bottle (12 ounces) amber ale or beer**
- 1 **onion, thinly sliced**
- 2 **tablespoons packed light brown sugar**
- 2 **tablespoons red wine or cider vinegar**
- **Spicy brown mustard**
- **Cocktail rye bread**

1. Combine bratwurst, ale, onion, brown sugar and vinegar in **CROCK-POT®** slow cooker. Cover; cook on LOW 4 to 5 hours.

2. Remove bratwurst from cooking liquid. Cut into ½-inch-thick slices.

3. Spread mustard on cocktail rye bread. Top with bratwurst slices and onion. (Whole brats also can be served on toasted split French or Italian rolls.)

Makes 30 to 36 appetizers

Tip: Choose a light-tasting beer when cooking brats. Hearty ales can leave the meat tasting slightly bitter.

Easiest Three-Cheese Fondue

- 2 cups (8 ounces) shredded mild or sharp Cheddar cheese
- 3/4 cup reduced-fat (2%) milk
- 1/2 cup (2 ounces) crumbled blue cheese
- 1 package (3 ounces) cream cheese, cut into cubes
- 1/4 cup finely chopped onion
- 1 tablespoon all-purpose flour
- 1 tablespoon butter or margarine
- 2 cloves garlic, minced
- 4 to 6 drops hot pepper sauce
- 1/8 teaspoon ground red pepper
- Breadsticks and assorted fresh vegetables for dipping

1. Combine all ingredients, except breadsticks and vegetables, in **CROCK-POT®** slow cooker. Cover; cook on LOW 2 to 2½ hours, stirring once or twice, until cheeses are melted and smooth.

2. Turn **CROCK-POT®** slow cooker to HIGH. Cook 1 to 1½ hours or until heated through. Serve with breadsticks and fresh vegetables for dipping.

Makes 8 servings

Tip: To reduce the total fat in this recipe, replace the Cheddar cheese and cream cheese with reduced-fat Cheddar and cream cheeses.

Reuben Dip

- 1 jar or bag (about 32 ounces) sauerkraut, drained
- 2 cups (8 ounces) shredded Swiss cheese
- 3 packages (2½ ounces each) corned beef, shredded
- ½ cup (1 stick) margarine, melted
- 1 egg, beaten
- Rye cocktail bread or crackers

1. Combine all ingredients except rye bread in **CROCK-POT®** slow cooker. Cover; cook on HIGH 2 hours.

2. Serve with rye cocktail bread or crackers.

Makes 12 servings

Note: Sauerkraut, a popular German food, is chopped or shredded cabbage that is salted and fermented in its own juice. Sauerkraut is an essential ingredient in a Reuben sandwich.

Cranberry-Barbecue Chicken Wings

- 3 pounds chicken wings, tips removed and split at the joint
- Salt and pepper
- 1 jar (12 ounces) cranberry-orange relish
- 1/2 cup barbecue sauce
- 2 tablespoons quick-cooking tapioca
- 1 tablespoon prepared mustard
- Orange slices (optional)

1. Preheat broiler. Place chicken on rack in broiler pan; season with salt and pepper. Broil 4 to 5 inches from heat for 10 to 12 minutes or until browned, turning once. Transfer chicken to **CROCK-POT®** slow cooker.

2. Combine relish, barbecue sauce, tapioca and mustard in small bowl. Pour over chicken. Cover; cook on LOW 4 to 5 hours. Serve with orange slices, if desired.

Makes about 16 appetizer servings

Barbecue Roast Beef

- 2 pounds boneless cooked roast beef
- 1 bottle (12 ounces) barbecue sauce
- 1½ cups water
- 10 to 12 sandwich rolls, halved

1. Combine roast beef, barbecue sauce and water in **CROCK-POT®** slow cooker. Cover; cook on LOW 2 hours.

2. Remove beef from **CROCK-POT®** slow cooker. Shred with two forks. Return beef to sauce; mix well. Serve on rolls.

Makes 10 to 12 sandwiches

Tip: Freeze leftovers as individual portions; just reheat in the microwave for fast meals!

Moroccan Spiced Chicken Wings

- **1/4 cup orange juice**
- **3 tablespoons tomato paste**
- **2 teaspoons ground cumin**
- **1 teaspoon curry powder**
- **1 teaspoon ground turmeric**
- **1/2 teaspoon ground cinnamon**
- **1/2 teaspoon ground ginger**
- **1 teaspoon salt**
- **1 tablespoon olive oil**
- **5 pounds chicken wings, tips removed and split at the joint**

1. Whisk orange juice, tomato paste, cumin, curry powder, turmeric, cinnamon, ginger and salt in large bowl; set aside.

2. Heat oil in large nonstick skillet over medium-high heat. Add wings and brown in several batches, about 6 minutes per batch. Transfer wings to bowl with sauce as they are cooked. Toss well to coat.

3. Place wings in **CROCK-POT®** slow cooker. Cover; cook on LOW 6 to 7 hours or on HIGH 3 to 3½ hours, or until tender.

Makes 8 servings

Parmesan Potato Wedges 

- 2 pounds red potatoes, cut into 1/2-inch wedges
- 1/4 cup finely chopped yellow onion
- 1 1/2 teaspoons dried oregano
- 1/2 teaspoon salt
- 1/4 teaspoon black pepper, or to taste
- 2 tablespoons butter, cut into small pieces
- 1/4 cup (1 ounce) grated Parmesan cheese

Layer potatoes, onion, oregano, salt, pepper and butter in **CROCK-POT®** slow cooker. Cover; cook on HIGH 4 hours. Transfer potatoes to serving platter and sprinkle with cheese.

Makes 6 servings

Easy Dirty Rice

- 1/2 pound bulk Italian sausage
- 2 cups water
- 1 cup uncooked long grain rice
- 1 onion, finely chopped
- 1 green bell pepper, finely chopped
- 1/2 cup finely chopped celery
- 1 1/2 teaspoons salt
- 1/2 teaspoon ground red pepper
- 1/2 cup chopped fresh parsley

1. Brown sausage 6 to 8 minutes in large skillet over medium-high heat, stirring to break up meat. Drain fat. Place sausage in **CROCK-POT®** slow cooker.

2. Stir in all remaining ingredients except parsley. Cover; cook on LOW 2 hours. Stir in parsley.

Makes 4 servings

Best Asian-Style Ribs

- **2 racks baby back pork ribs, split into 3 sections each**
- **6 ounces hoisin sauce**
- **½ cup maraschino cherries**
- **½ cup rice wine vinegar**
- **2 tablespoons minced fresh ginger**
- **4 green onions, chopped (optional)**

1. Combine ribs, hoisin sauce, cherries, vinegar and ginger in **CROCK-POT®** slow cooker. Add enough water to cover ribs.

2. Cover; cook on LOW 6 to 7 hours or on HIGH 3 to 3½ hours, or until pork is done. Sprinkle with green onions before serving, if desired.

Makes 6 to 8 servings

Pizza Fondue

- ½ pound bulk Italian sausage
- 1 cup chopped onion
- 2 jars (26 ounces each) meatless pasta sauce
- 4 ounces thinly sliced ham, finely chopped
- 1 package (3 ounces) sliced pepperoni, finely chopped
- ¼ teaspoon red pepper flakes
- 1 pound mozzarella cheese, cut into ¾-inch cubes
- 1 loaf Italian or French bread, cut into 1-inch cubes

1. Cook and stir sausage and onion in large skillet over medium-high heat until sausage is browned. Drain and discard fat.

2. Transfer sausage mixture to **CROCK-POT®** slow cooker. Stir in pasta sauce, ham, pepperoni and red pepper flakes. Cover; cook on LOW 3 to 4 hours. Serve warm fondue with mozzarella cheese and bread cubes.

Makes 20 to 25 servings

Big Al's Hot and Sweet Sausage Sandwich

- 4 to 5 pounds hot Italian sausage links
- 1 jar (26 ounces) pasta sauce
- 1 Vidalia onion, sliced
- 1 green bell pepper, sliced
- 1 red bell pepper, sliced
- 1/4 cup packed dark brown sugar
- Italian rolls, cut in half
- Provolone cheese, sliced (optional)

1. Combine sausages, pasta sauce, onion, bell peppers and brown sugar in **CROCK-POT®** slow cooker. Cover; cook on LOW 8 to 10 hours or on HIGH 4 to 6 hours.

2. Place sausages on rolls. Top with vegetable mixture. Add provolone cheese, if desired.

Makes 8 to 10 servings

Chunky Pinto Bean Dip

- 1 tablespoon olive oil
- 2 cloves garlic, minced
- 1/2 teaspoon ground cumin
- 1 can (about 10 ounces) diced tomatoes with green chiles
- 1/2 can (about 15 ounces) pinto beans, rinsed and drained
- 2 tablespoons whipping cream
- 1/2 cup (about 2 ounces) shredded sharp Cheddar cheese
- 1/4 cup chopped fresh cilantro

1. Heat oil in medium saucepan over medium heat. Add garlic and cumin and cook 15 seconds, stirring constantly.

2. Drain tomatoes with chiles, reserving one-fourth canning liquid. Add tomatoes with chiles and reserved liquid to saucepan. Stir in beans.

3. Increase heat to medium-high. Bring to a boil and cook 1 minute. Reduce to medium-low. Partially mash with potato masher. Remove from heat. Add cream, cheese and cilantro; stir until cheese is melted.

4. Coat **CROCK-POT® LITTLE DIPPER®** slow cooker with nonstick cooking spray. Fill with prepared dip.

Makes 1 3/4 cups

Warm Spiced Apples and Pears

- 1/2 cup (1 stick) unsalted butter
- 1 vanilla bean
- 1 cup packed brown sugar
- 1/2 cup water
- 1/2 lemon, sliced
- 1 cinnamon stick, broken in half
- 1/2 teaspoon ground cloves
- 5 pears, quartered and cored
- 5 Granny Smith apples, quartered and cored

1. Melt butter in saucepan over medium heat. Cut vanilla bean in half and scrape out seeds. Add seeds and bean to pan with brown sugar, water, lemon slices, cinnamon stick and cloves. Bring to a boil; cook and stir 1 minute. Remove from heat.

2. Combine pears, apples and butter mixture in **CROCK-POT®** slow cooker; mix well. Cover; cook on LOW 3½ to 4 hours or on HIGH 2 hours. Stir every 45 minutes to ensure even cooking. Remove vanilla bean before serving.

Makes 6 servings

Decadent Chocolate Delight

- 1 package (about 18 ounces) chocolate cake mix
- 1 container (8 ounces) sour cream
- 1 cup semisweet chocolate chips
- 1 cup water
- 4 eggs
- 3/4 cup vegetable oil
- 1 package (4-serving size) instant chocolate pudding and pie filling mix
- Vanilla ice cream

1. Coat **CROCK-POT®** slow cooker with nonstick cooking spray.

2. Combine all ingredients except ice cream in medium bowl; mix well. Transfer to **CROCK-POT®** slow cooker.

3. Cover; cook on LOW 3 to 4 hours or on HIGH 1½ to 1¾ hours. Serve hot or warm with ice cream.

Makes 12 servings

Herbed Fall Vegetables

- 2 Yukon Gold potatoes, peeled and cut into 1/2-inch dice
- 2 sweet potatoes, peeled and cut into 1/2-inch dice
- 3 parsnips, peeled and cut into 1/2-inch dice
- 1 fennel bulb, sliced and cut into 1/2-inch dice
- 1/2 to 3/4 cup chopped fresh herbs, such as tarragon, parsley, sage or thyme
- 1/4 cup (1/2 stick) butter, cut into small pieces
- 1 cup chicken broth
- 1 tablespoon Dijon mustard
- 1 tablespoon salt
- Black pepper

1. Combine potatoes, sweet potatoes, parsnips, fennel, herbs and butter in **CROCK-POT®** slow cooker.

2. Whisk together broth, mustard, salt and pepper in small bowl. Pour mixture over vegetables. Cover; cook on LOW 4½ hours or on HIGH 3 hours, or until vegetables are tender, stirring occasionally to ensure even cooking.

Makes 6 servings

Mexican Cheese Soup

- 1 pound pasteurized process cheese product, cubed
- 1 pound ground beef, cooked and drained
- 1 can (about 15 ounces) kidney beans, undrained
- 1 can (about 14 ounces) diced tomatoes with green chiles, undrained
- 1 can (about 14 ounces) stewed tomatoes, undrained
- 1 can ($8\frac{3}{4}$ ounces) whole kernel corn, undrained
- 1 envelope taco seasoning
- 1 jalapeño pepper, diced* (optional)
- Corn chips (optional)

**Jalapeño peppers can sting and irritate the skin, so wear rubber gloves when handling peppers and do not touch your eyes.*

1. Coat inside of **CROCK-POT®** slow cooker with nonstick cooking spray. Add cheese, beef, beans, tomatoes with chiles, stewed tomatoes with juice, corn, taco seasoning and jalapeño, if desired. Mix well.

2. Cover; cook on LOW 4 to 5 hours or on HIGH 3 hours. Serve with corn chips, if desired.

Makes 6 to 8 servings

Chili with Chocolate

- 1 pound ground beef
- 1 onion, chopped
- 3 cloves garlic, minced, divided
- 1 can (about 28 ounces) diced tomatoes
- 1 can (about 15 ounces) chili beans in mild or spicy sauce
- 2 tablespoons chili powder
- 1 tablespoon grated semisweet baking chocolate
- $1\frac{1}{2}$ teaspoons ground cumin
- $\frac{1}{2}$ teaspoon salt
- $\frac{1}{2}$ teaspoon black pepper
- $\frac{1}{2}$ teaspoon hot pepper sauce

1. Brown beef, onion and one-third garlic in large nonstick skillet over medium-high heat, stirring to break up meat. Drain fat.

2. Place beef mixture in **CROCK-POT®** slow cooker. Stir in tomatoes, beans, chili powder, chocolate and remaining garlic.

3. Cover; cook on LOW 5 to 6 hours. Stir in cumin, salt, black pepper and hot pepper sauce during last hour of cooking.

Makes 4 servings

Blue Cheese Potatoes

- 2 pounds red potatoes, peeled and cut into 1/2-inch pieces
- 1 1/4 cups chopped green onions, divided
- 2 tablespoons olive oil, divided
- 1 teaspoon dried basil
- 1/2 teaspoon salt
- 1/4 teaspoon black pepper
- 1/2 cup crumbled blue cheese

1. Layer potatoes, 1 cup green onions, 1 tablespoon oil, basil, salt and pepper in **CROCK-POT®** slow cooker. Cover; cook on LOW 7 hours or on HIGH 4 hours.

2. Turn **CROCK-POT®** slow cooker to HIGH. Gently stir in cheese and remaining 1 tablespoon oil. Cook 5 minutes longer to allow flavors to blend. Transfer potatoes to serving platter and top with remaining 1/4 cup green onions.

Makes 5 servings

Patio Parties

Corn on the Cob with Garlic Herb Butter

- **½ cup (1 stick) unsalted butter, softened**
- **3 to 4 cloves garlic, minced**
- **2 tablespoons finely minced fresh parsley**
- **4 to 5 ears of corn, husked**
- **Salt and black pepper**

1. Combine butter, garlic and parsley in small bowl.

2. Place each ear of corn on a piece of aluminum foil and generously spread with butter mixture. Season with salt and pepper and tightly seal foil. Place in **CROCK-POT®** slow cooker; overlap ears, if necessary. Add enough water to come one fourth of the way up ears.

3. Cover; cook on LOW 4 to 5 hours or on HIGH 2 to 2½ hours.

Makes 4 to 5 servings

Cod Tapenade

4 cod fillets, or other firm white fish (2 to 3 pounds total)
Salt and black pepper
2 lemons, thinly sliced
Tapenade (recipe follows)

1. Season fish with salt and pepper.

2. Arrange half of lemon slices in bottom of **CROCK-POT®** slow cooker. Top with fish. Cover fish with remaining lemon slices. Cover; cook on HIGH 1 hour or until fish is just cooked through (actual time depends on thickness of fish).

3. Remove fish to serving plates; discard lemon. Top with Tapenade.

Makes 4 servings

Tapenade

1/2 pound pitted kalamata olives
2 tablespoons anchovy paste
2 tablespoons capers, drained
1 clove garlic
1/8 teaspoon ground red pepper
1/4 teaspoon grated orange peel
2 tablespoons chopped fresh thyme or Italian parsley
1/2 cup olive oil

Place all ingredients except oil in food processor. Pulse to roughly chop. Add oil and pulse briefly to form a chunky paste.

Makes 4 servings

Tip: In a hurry? Substitute store-brought tapenade for homemade!

Confetti Black Beans

- **1 cup dried black beans**
- **$1\frac{1}{2}$ teaspoons olive oil**
- **1 onion, chopped**
- **$\frac{1}{4}$ cup chopped red bell pepper**
- **$\frac{1}{4}$ cup chopped yellow bell pepper**
- **1 jalapeño pepper, finely chopped***
- **1 tomato, seeded and chopped**
- **$\frac{1}{2}$ teaspoon salt**
- **$\frac{1}{8}$ teaspoon black pepper**
- **2 cloves garlic, minced**
- **1 can (about 14 ounces) chicken broth**
- **1 bay leaf**
- **Hot pepper sauce (optional)**

Jalapeño peppers can sting and irritate the skin, so wear rubber gloves when handling peppers and do not touch your eyes.

1. Soak beans in water in large bowl 8 hours or overnight. Drain.

2. Heat oil in large skillet over medium heat. Add onion, bell peppers and jalapeño; cook and stir 5 minutes or until onion is tender. Add tomato, salt and black pepper; cook 5 minutes. Stir in garlic.

3. Place beans, broth and bay leaf in **CROCK-POT®** slow cooker. Add onion mixture to beans. Cover; cook on LOW 7 to 8 hours or on HIGH $4\frac{1}{2}$ to 5 hours, or until beans are tender. Remove and discard bay leaf before serving. Serve with hot pepper sauce, if desired.

Makes 6 servings

Fruit Ambrosia with Dumplings

- **4 cups fresh or frozen fruit, cut into bite-size pieces***
- **1/2 cup plus 2 tablespoons granulated sugar, divided**
- **1/2 cup warm apple or cran-apple juice**
- **2 tablespoons quick-cooking tapioca**
- **1 cup all-purpose flour**
- **1 1/4 teaspoons baking powder**
- **1/4 teaspoon salt**
- **3 tablespoons butter or margarine, cut into small pieces**
- **1/2 cup milk**
- **1 large egg**
- **2 tablespoons packed light brown sugar, plus more for garnish**
- **Vanilla ice cream, whipped cream or fruity yogurt (optional)**

Use strawberries, raspberries or peaches.

1. Combine fruit, 1/2 cup granulated sugar, juice and tapioca in **CROCK-POT®** slow cooker. Cover; cook on LOW 5 to 6 hours or on HIGH 2 1/2 to 3 hours or until thick sauce forms.

2. Combine flour, remaining 2 tablespoons granulated sugar, baking powder and salt in medium bowl. Cut in butter using pastry cutter or two knives until mixture resembles coarse crumbs. Whisk milk and egg in small bowl. Pour milk mixture into flour mixture. Stir until soft dough forms.

3. Turn **CROCK-POT®** slow cooker to HIGH. Drop dough by teaspoonfuls on top of fruit. Sprinkle with 2 tablespoons brown sugar. Cover; cook on HIGH 30 minutes to 1 hour or until toothpick inserted in dumplings comes out clean.

4. Sprinkle dumplings with additional brown sugar, if desired. Serve warm with ice cream, whipped cream or yogurt.

Makes 4 to 6 servings

Patio Parties

Spicy Beans Tex-Mex

- 1 1/3 cups water
- 1/3 cup lentils
- 5 strips bacon
- 1 onion, chopped
- 1 can (about 15 ounces) pinto beans, rinsed and drained
- 1 can (about 15 ounces) red kidney beans, rinsed and drained
- 1 can (about 14 ounces) diced tomatoes
- 3 tablespoons ketchup
- 3 cloves garlic, minced
- 1 teaspoon chili powder
- 1/2 teaspoon ground cumin
- 1/4 teaspoon red pepper flakes
- 1 bay leaf

1. Combine water and lentils in large saucepan. Boil 20 to 30 minutes; drain.

2. Cook bacon in medium skillet until crisp. Drain on paper towels. Cool, then crumble bacon. Cook onion in bacon drippings until tender.

3. Combine lentils, bacon, onion, beans, tomatoes, ketchup, garlic, chili powder, cumin, red pepper flakes and bay leaf in **CROCK-POT®** slow cooker. Cover; cook on LOW 5 to 6 hours or on HIGH 3 to 4 hours. Remove bay leaf before serving.

Makes 8 to 10 servings

Dulce de Leche

- 1 can (14 ounces) sweetened condensed milk

1. Pour milk into 9×5-inch loaf pan. Cover tightly with aluminum foil. Place loaf pan in **CROCK-POT®** slow cooker. Pour enough water to reach halfway up sides of loaf pan. Cover; cook on LOW 5 to 6 hours or until golden and thickened.

2. Coat **CROCK-POT® LITTLE DIPPER®** slow cooker with nonstick cooking spray. Fill with warm dip.

Makes about 1 1/2 cups

Spicy Beans Tex-Mex

Steamed Southern Sweet Potato Custard

- 1 can (16 ounces) cut sweet potatoes, drained
- 1 can (12 ounces) evaporated milk, divided
- ½ cup packed light brown sugar
- 2 eggs, lightly beaten
- 1 teaspoon ground cinnamon
- ½ teaspoon ground ginger
- ¼ teaspoon salt
- Whipped cream
- Ground nutmeg

1. Place rack in **CROCK-POT®** slow cooker and pour in 2 cups water.

2. Process sweet potatoes with ¼ cup evaporated milk in food processor or blender until smooth. Add remaining evaporated milk, brown sugar, eggs, cinnamon, ginger and salt; process until well blended. Pour into ungreased 1-quart soufflé dish. Cover tightly with foil. Place dish on rack in **CROCK-POT®** slow cooker. Cover; cook on HIGH 2½ to 3 hours or until skewer inserted into center comes out clean.

3. Transfer dish to wire rack. Uncover; let stand 30 minutes. Garnish with whipped cream and nutmeg.

Makes 4 servings

Quinoa and Vegetable Medley

- 2 sweet potatoes, cut into 1/2-inch-thick slices
- 1 eggplant, peeled and cut into 1/2-inch cubes
- 1 tomato, cut into wedges
- 1 green bell pepper, sliced
- 1 onion, cut into wedges
- 1/2 teaspoon salt
- 1/4 teaspoon black pepper
- 1/4 teaspoon ground red pepper
- 1 cup uncooked quinoa
- 2 cups vegetable broth
- 2 cloves garlic, minced
- 1/2 teaspoon dried thyme
- 1/4 teaspoon dried marjoram

1. Spray **CROCK-POT®** slow cooker with cooking spray. Combine sweet potatoes, eggplant, tomato, bell pepper and onion and toss with salt, black pepper and red pepper in **CROCK-POT®** slow cooker.

2. Meanwhile, place quinoa in strainer; rinse well. Add to vegetable mixture. Stir in broth, garlic, thyme and marjoram. Cover; cook on LOW for 5 hours or on HIGH for 2½ hours, or until quinoa is tender and broth is absorbed.

Makes 6 servings

Fiesta Dip

- 8 ounces canned refried beans
- 1/2 cup shredded Cheddar cheese, plus additional for garnish
- 1/4 cup salsa
- 1/3 cup green chile pepper, chopped (optional)
- Tortilla or corn chips (optional)
- Chopped tomatoes (optional)

1. Combine all ingredients and place in **CROCK-POT® LITTLE DIPPER®** slow cooker. Cover; heat for 45 minutes or until cheese is melted, stirring occasionally.

2. Serve with tortilla chips or corn chips. Garnish with chopped tomatoes and Cheddar cheese.

Makes 16 servings

Risotto-Style Peppered Rice

- 1 cup uncooked converted long grain rice
- 1 green bell pepper, chopped
- 1 red bell pepper, chopped
- 1 cup chopped onion
- 1/2 teaspoon ground turmeric
- 1/8 teaspoon ground red pepper (optional)
- 1 can (about 14 ounces) chicken broth
- 4 ounces Monterey Jack cheese with jalapeño peppers, cubed
- 1/2 cup milk
- 1/4 cup (1/2 stick) butter, cut into small pieces
- 1 teaspoon salt

1. Place rice, bell peppers, onion, turmeric and red pepper, if desired, in **CROCK-POT®** slow cooker. Stir in broth. Cover; cook on LOW 4 to 5 hours or until rice is tender and broth is absorbed.

2. Stir in cheese, milk, butter and salt; fluff rice with fork. Cover; cook on LOW 5 minutes or until cheese is melted.

Makes 4 to 6 servings

Tip: Dairy products should be added at the end of the cooking time because they will curdle if cooked in the **CROCK-POT®** slow cooker for a long time.

Pear Crunch

- 1 can (8 ounces) crushed pineapple in juice, undrained
- 1/4 cup pineapple or apple juice
- 3 tablespoons dried cranberries
- 1 1/2 teaspoons quick-cooking tapioca
- 1/4 teaspoon vanilla
- 2 pears, cored and halved
- 1/4 cup granola with almonds
- Mint leaves (optional)

1. Combine pineapple with juice, 1/4 cup pineapple juice, cranberries, tapioca and vanilla in **CROCK-POT®** slow cooker; mix well. Place pears cut side down on pineapple mixture.

2. Cover; cook on LOW 3 1/2 to 4 1/2 hours. Arrange pear halves on serving plates. Spoon pineapple mixture over pear halves. Sprinkle with granola. Garnish with mint leaves.

Makes 4 servings

Spiced Apple Tea

3 bags cinnamon herbal tea

3 cups boiling water

2 cups unsweetened apple juice

6 whole cloves

1 cinnamon stick

Place tea bags in **CROCK-POT®** slow cooker. Pour boiling water over tea bags; cover and let stand 10 minutes. Remove and discard tea bags. Add apple juice, cloves and cinnamon stick to **CROCK-POT®** slow cooker. Cover; cook on LOW 2 to 3 hours. Remove and discard cloves and cinnamon stick. Serve warm in mugs.

Makes 4 servings

Onion Marmalade

- 1 bottle (12 ounces) balsamic vinegar
- 1 bottle (12 ounces) white wine vinegar
- 3 tablespoons cornstarch or arrowroot
- 2 tablespoons water
- 1½ cups packed dark brown sugar
- 2 teaspoons cumin seeds
- 2 teaspoons coriander seeds
- 4 large yellow onions, halved and thinly sliced

1. Cook vinegars in large saucepan over high heat until reduced to ¼ cup. Sauce will be thick and syrupy. Remove from heat. Blend cornstarch and water in small cup. Add brown sugar, cumin, coriander seeds and cornstarch mixture to sauce; blend well.

2. Place onions in **CROCK-POT®** slow cooker. Stir in sauce; mix well. Cover; cook on LOW 8 to 10 hours or HIGH 4 to 6 hours, or until onions are no longer crunchy. Stir occasionally to prevent sticking. Store in refrigerator for up to two weeks.

Makes 5 cups

Tip: Serve as side dish or condiment with eggs, roasted vegetables and meats, or on sandwiches.

Barley Salad

- 2 onions, chopped
- 2 sweet potatoes, peeled and chopped
- 1 cup pearl barley
- 1 teaspoon salt
- 1/2 teaspoon cinnamon
- 1/4 teaspoon ground red pepper (optional)
- 1 1/2 cups water
- 2 apples, peeled and chopped
- 1 cup dried cranberries
- 1 cup chopped pecans

1. Spread onions and sweet potatoes on bottom of **CROCK-POT®** slow cooker. Add barley, salt, cinnamon and red pepper, if desired. Pour in water. Cook on LOW 4 hours or on HIGH 2 hours.

2. Stir in apples, cranberries and pecans. Serve warm or at room temperature.

Makes 16 servings

Milk and Honey Corn Pudding

- **3 ounces cream cheese**
- **2 tablespoons butter, cut into small pieces**
- **1 cup evaporated milk**
- **3 eggs**
- **1/3 cup honey**
- **2 cans (about 15 ounces each) cream-style corn**
- **1 can (16 ounces) corn**
- **1 teaspoon salt**
- **1 package (8 1/2 ounces) corn muffin mix**

1. Grease **CROCK-POT®** slow cooker.

2. Place cream cheese in large microwavable bowl. Microwave 30 seconds on HIGH or until melted. Add butter; stir until butter is melted and mixture is creamy. Whisk in evaporated milk, eggs and honey. Stir in creamed corn, corn and salt. Stir in muffin mix.

3. Pour batter into **CROCK-POT®** slow cooker. Cover, cook on LOW 4 1/2 hours or until pudding is golden and a knife inserted into the center comes out clean. Let rest 10 minutes before serving.

Makes 8 servings

Coconut-Lime Sweet Potatoes with Walnuts

- **2½ pounds sweet potatoes, peeled and cut into 1-inch pieces**
- **8 ounces shredded peeled carrots**
- **¾ cup sweetened coconut flakes, divided**
- **¼ cup (½ stick) butter, melted**
- **3 tablespoons sugar**
- **½ teaspoon salt**
- **¾ cup walnuts, toasted and coarsely chopped, divided**
- **2 teaspoons grated lime peel**

1. Combine sweet potatoes, carrots, ½ cup coconut, butter, sugar and salt in **CROCK-POT®** slow cooker. Cover; cook on LOW 5 to 6 hours until sweet potatoes are tender.

2. Place remaining ¼ cup coconut in small nonstick skillet. Cook over low heat 4 minutes or until coconut is lightly browned, stirring constantly. Transfer to a small bowl and cool completely.

3. Mash sweet potatoes. Stir in 3 tablespoons walnuts and lime peel. Sprinkle top of mashed sweet potatoes with remaining walnuts and coconut.

Makes 6 to 8 servings

Baked Beans

- 2 cans (about 15 ounces each) baked beans
- 1 cup ketchup
- 1/2 cup barbecue sauce
- 1/2 cup packed brown sugar
- 5 slices bacon, chopped
- 1/2 green bell pepper, chopped
- 1/2 onion, chopped
- 1 1/2 teaspoons prepared mustard
- Fresh parsley (optional)

Place all ingredients except parsley in **CROCK-POT®** slow cooker. Stir well to combine. Cover; cook on LOW 8 to 12 hours or on HIGH 3 to 4 hours. Garnish with fresh parsley.

Makes 6 to 8 servings

Lemon and Tangerine Glazed Carrots

- 6 cups sliced carrots
- 1½ cups apple juice
- 6 tablespoons butter
- ¼ cup packed brown sugar
- 2 tablespoons grated lemon peel
- 2 tablespoons grated tangerine peel
- ½ teaspoon salt
- Chopped fresh parsley (optional)

Combine all ingredients except parsley in **CROCK-POT®** slow cooker. Cover; cook on LOW 4 to 5 hours or on HIGH 1 to 3 hours. Garnish with chopped parsley.

Makes 10 to 12 servings

Garlic and Herb Polenta

3 tablespoons butter, divided

8 cups water

2 cups yellow cornmeal

2 teaspoons finely minced garlic

2 teaspoons salt

3 tablespoons chopped fresh herbs such as parsley, chives, thyme or chervil (or a combination)

1. Grease **CROCK-POT®** slow cooker with 1 tablespoon butter. Add water, cornmeal, garlic, salt and remaining 2 tablespoons butter; stir.

2. Cover; cook on LOW 4 hours or on HIGH 3 hours, stirring occasionally. Stir in chopped herbs just before serving.

Makes 6 servings

Tip: Polenta may also be poured into a greased pan and allowed to cool until set. Cut into squares (or slice as desired) to serve. For even more great flavor, chill polenta slices until firm, then grill or fry until golden brown.

Mediterranean Red Potatoes

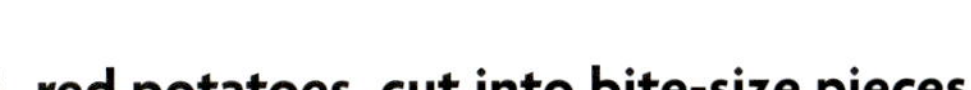

- **3 red potatoes, cut into bite-size pieces**
- **2/3 cup fresh or frozen pearl onions**
- **Garlic-flavored cooking spray**
- **3/4 teaspoon dried Italian seasoning**
- **1/4 teaspoon black pepper**
- **1 tomato, chopped**
- **2 ounces (1/2 cup) feta cheese, crumbled**
- **2 tablespoons chopped black olives**

1. Place potatoes and onions in $1\frac{1}{2}$-quart soufflé dish. Spray with cooking spray; toss to coat. Add Italian seasoning and pepper; mix well. Cover dish tightly with foil.

2. Tear off three 18×3-inch strips of heavy-duty foil. Cross strips to resemble wheel spokes. Place soufflé dish in center of strips. Pull foil strips up and over dish and place dish into **CROCK-POT®** slow cooker.

3. Pour hot water into **CROCK-POT®** slow cooker to about $1\frac{1}{2}$ inches from top of soufflé dish. Cover; cook on LOW 7 to 8 hours.

4. Use foil handles to lift dish out of **CROCK-POT®** slow cooker. Stir in tomato, cheese and olives.

Makes 4 servings

Bananas Foster 

- 12 bananas, cut into quarters
- 1 cup flaked coconut
- 1 cup dark corn syrup
- 2/3 cup butter, melted
- 1/4 cup lemon juice
- 2 teaspoons grated lemon peel
- 2 teaspoons rum
- 1 teaspoon ground cinnamon
- 1/2 teaspoon salt
- 12 slices pound cake
- 1 quart vanilla ice cream

Combine bananas and coconut in **CROCK-POT®** slow cooker. Stir together corn syrup, butter, lemon juice, lemon peel, rum, cinnamon and salt in medium bowl; pour over bananas. Cover; cook on LOW 1 to 2 hours. Arrange bananas on pound cake slices. Top with ice cream and warm sauce.

Makes 12 servings

Chunky Ranch Potatoes

- 3 pounds unpeeled red potatoes, quartered
- 1 cup water
- 1/2 cup prepared ranch dressing
- 1/2 cup grated Parmesan or Cheddar cheese (optional)
- 1/4 cup minced fresh chives

1. Place potatoes in **CROCK-POT®** slow cooker. Add water. Cover; cook on LOW 7 to 9 hours or on HIGH 4 to 6 hours, or until potatoes are tender.

2. Stir in ranch dressing, cheese, if desired, and chives. Break potatoes into chunks. Serve hot or cold.

Makes 8 servings

Red Pepper Relish

- 4 red bell peppers, cut into thin strips
- 2 Vidalia or other sweet onions, thinly sliced
- 6 tablespoons cider vinegar
- 1/4 cup packed light brown sugar
- 2 tablespoons vegetable oil
- 2 tablespoons honey
- 1/2 teaspoon salt
- 1/2 teaspoon dried thyme
- 1/2 teaspoon red pepper flakes
- 1/2 teaspoon black pepper
- 2 baguettes, sliced and toasted

Combine all ingredients except baguettes in **CROCK-POT®** slow cooker; mix well. Cover; cook on LOW 4 hours. Serve relish on toasted baguette slices.

Makes 8 servings

Scalloped Tomatoes and Corn

1 can (about 15 ounces) cream-style corn
1 can (about 14 ounces) diced tomatoes
3/4 cup saltine or soda cracker crumbs
1 egg, lightly beaten
2 teaspoons sugar
3/4 teaspoon black pepper
Chopped fresh tomatoes
Chopped fresh parsley

Combine corn, tomatoes, cracker crumbs, egg, sugar and pepper in **CROCK-POT®** slow cooker; mix well. Cover; cook on LOW 4 to 6 hours. Sprinkle with chopped tomatoes and parsley before serving.

Makes 4 to 6 servings

Note: Fresh tomatoes are available all year, although locally grown summer tomatoes are superior to all others. Depending on the area, tomato season usually begins in mid-summer and lasts through September.

Family Get-Togethers

Easy Mu Shu Pork

1 package (14 ounces) coleslaw mix, divided
1 package (10 ounces) shredded carrots, divided
1 package (6 ounces) shiitake mushrooms, sliced
3 cloves garlic, minced
3/4 cup hoisin sauce, divided
3 tablespoons reduced-sodium soy sauce
3/4 pound pork loin roast
12 (6-inch) tortillas
1 bunch green onions, chopped (optional)
2 tablespoons sesame oil (optional)

1. Place half each of coleslaw mix and carrots in **CROCK-POT®** slow cooker. Add mushrooms; toss to combine. Stir in garlic. Add 1/2 cup hoisin sauce and soy sauce; stir to combine. Place pork on top of vegetables. Cover; cook on LOW 4 to 5 hours or until pork is fork-tender.

2. Shred pork with two forks. Add remaining half each of coleslaw mix and carrots, and remaining 1/4 cup hoisin sauce; stir to combine.

3. Warm tortillas according to package directions. Divide pork mixture among tortillas. Top with green onions and sesame oil, if desired.

Makes 6 servings

New England Chuck Roast

- 1 beef chuck roast (4 to 5 pounds), string on
- 2 teaspoons salt
- 1/4 teaspoon black pepper
- Olive oil
- 4 cups water, divided
- 2 cups carrots, cut into 2-inch pieces
- 2 stalks celery, cut into 1-inch pieces
- 1 1/2 cups yellow onion, cut into quarters
- 4 red potatoes, cut into quarters
- 3 bay leaves
- 2 tablespoons white vinegar
- 2 tablespoons horseradish
- 1 head cabbage, cut into quarters or eighths
- 4 tablespoons all-purpose flour
- 2 tablespoons cornstarch

1. Season roast with salt and pepper. Heat oil in large skillet over medium heat. Brown roast on all sides. Transfer to **CROCK-POT®** slow cooker.

2. Add 3 cups water, carrots, celery, onion, potatoes, bay leaves, vinegar and horseradish to **CROCK-POT®** slow cooker. Cover; cook on LOW 5 to 7 hours or on HIGH 2 to 4 hours.

3. Add cabbage to **CROCK-POT®** slow cooker one hour before serving. Combine flour and cornstarch with remaining 1 cup water in small bowl. Stir into **CROCK-POT®** slow cooker. Cover; turn **CROCK-POT®** slow cooker to HIGH and cook for 1 hour or until sauce is thickened. Season with salt and pepper. Remove and discard bay leaves before serving. Serve roast with sauce and vegetables.

Makes 8 servings

Indian-Style Apricot Chicken

- 6 skinless chicken thighs, rinsed and patted dry (see Note)
- 1/4 teaspoon salt
- 1/4 teaspoon black pepper
- 1 tablespoon vegetable oil
- 1 onion, chopped
- 2 cloves garlic, minced
- 2 tablespoons grated fresh ginger
- 1/2 teaspoon ground cinnamon
- 1/8 teaspoon ground allspice
- 1 can (about 14 ounces) diced tomatoes
- 1 cup chicken broth
- 1 package (8 ounces) dried apricots
- Pinch saffron threads (optional)
- Hot basmati rice
- 2 tablespoons chopped fresh parsley (optional)

1. Coat **CROCK-POT®** slow cooker with nonstick cooking spray. Season chicken with salt and pepper. Heat oil in large skillet over medium-high heat. Brown chicken on all sides. Transfer to **CROCK-POT®** slow cooker.

2. Add onion to skillet. Cook and stir 3 to 5 minutes or until translucent. Stir in garlic, ginger, cinnamon and allspice. Cook and stir 15 to 30 seconds or until fragrant. Add tomatoes with juice and broth; cook 2 to 3 minutes or until heated through. Pour into **CROCK-POT®** slow cooker.

3. Add apricots and saffron, if desired. Cover; cook on LOW 5 to 6 hours or on HIGH 3 to 4 hours, or until chicken is tender. Add salt and pepper, if desired. Serve with rice and garnish with chopped parsley.

Makes 4 to 6 servings

Note: To skin chicken easily, grasp skin with paper towel and pull away. Repeat with fresh paper towel for each piece of chicken, discarding skins and towels.

Peppered Pork Cutlets with Onion Gravy

1/2 teaspoon paprika
1/4 teaspoon ground cumin
1/4 teaspoon black pepper
1/8 teaspoon ground red pepper (optional)
4 boneless pork cutlets (4 ounces each), trimmed of fat
2 cups thinly sliced onions
2 tablespoons all-purpose flour, divided
3/4 cup water
1 1/2 teaspoons chicken bouillon granules
2 tablespoons fat-free (skim) milk
1/4 teaspoon salt

1. Combine paprika, cumin, black pepper and red pepper, if desired, in small bowl; blend well. Sprinkle mixture evenly over one side of each cutlet and press down gently to adhere. Let stand 15 minutes to absorb flavors.

2. Heat large nonstick skillet over medium heat. Spray with nonstick cooking spray. Add pork, seasoned side down, and cook 3 minutes or until richly browned. Remove from skillet and transfer to **CROCK-POT®** slow cooker.

3. Coat skillet with cooking spray and heat over medium-high heat. Add onions; cook 4 minutes or until richly browned, stirring frequently. Sprinkle with 1½ tablespoons flour; toss to coat. Stir in water and bouillon; bring to a boil. Add onions and any accumulated juices to **CROCK-POT®** slow cooker; spoon some sauce over pork. Cover; cook on LOW 4 to 5 hours.

4. Place pork on serving platter and set aside. Turn **CROCK-POT®** slow cooker to HIGH. Stir milk into onion mixture, or, for thicker consistency, combine milk and remaining ½ tablespoon flour and add to onion mixture. Add salt and transfer to **CROCK-POT®** slow cooker. Cook 10 minutes or until thickened. Spoon sauce over and around pork.

Makes 4 servings

Green Onion-Bacon Creamed Corn

- 2 packages (12 ounces each) frozen corn
- 4 slices bacon, crisp-cooked and crumbled, divided
- 1 cup chopped green onions
- 3/4 cup whipping cream
- 4 teaspoons sugar
- 1/2 teaspoon salt

Generously grease **CROCK-POT®** slow cooker. Stir in corn, half of bacon, green onions, cream, sugar and salt. Cover; cook on LOW 4 to 4½ hours. Stir well. Garnish with remaining crumbled bacon.

Makes 8 servings

Cheesy Cauliflower

- **5 tablespoons unsalted butter**
- **1 cup finely chopped onion**
- **6 tablespoons all-purpose flour**
- **1/4 teaspoon dry mustard**
- **2 cups milk**
- **2 cups (about 8 ounces) shredded sharp Cheddar cheese**
- **1/2 teaspoon salt**
- **1/4 teaspoon black pepper**
- **3 pounds cauliflower florets**
- **1/4 cup water**

1. Melt butter in medium saucepan over medium-high heat. Add onion and cook 4 to 5 minutes until slightly softened. Add flour and mustard; cook and stir until well combined. Cook 3 minutes, stirring constantly. Whisk in milk until smooth. Bring to a boil; cook 1 to 2 minutes or until thickened. Stir in cheese, salt and pepper; stir until cheese is melted.

2. Generously grease **CROCK-POT®** slow cooker. Add cauliflower and water. Pour cheese mixture over top. Cover; cook on LOW 4 to 4½ hours or until cauliflower is crisp-tender.

Makes 8 to 10 servings

Super Easy Chicken Noodle Soup

- 1 can (about 48 ounces) chicken broth
- 2 boneless, skinless chicken breasts, cut into bite-size pieces
- 4 cups water
- 2/3 cup diced onion
- 2/3 cup diced celery
- 2/3 cup diced carrots
- 2/3 cup sliced mushrooms
- 1/2 cup frozen peas
- 4 chicken bouillon cubes
- 2 tablespoons butter
- 1 tablespoon dried parsley flakes
- 1 teaspoon salt
- 1 teaspoon ground cumin
- 1 teaspoon dried marjoram
- 1 teaspoon black pepper
- 2 cups cooked egg noodles

Combine all ingredients except noodles in **CROCK-POT®** slow cooker. Cover; cook on LOW 5 to 7 hours or on HIGH 3 to 4 hours. Stir in noodles 30 minutes before serving.

Makes 4 servings

Chicken Gumbo over Rice

- 4 tablespoons olive oil, divided
- 1/2 pound Italian sausage, cut into 1/4-inch slices
- 1/4 cup all-purpose flour
- 1 pound boneless, skinless chicken breasts, cut into 1/2-inch slices
- 1 cup chopped onions
- 1 cup chopped celery
- 1 cup diced green bell peppers
- 2 tablespoons minced jalapeño or serrano peppers*
- 1 teaspoon paprika
- 1 1/2 cups fresh or frozen okra, cut into 1/4-inch slices
- 1 cup chicken broth
- 1/2 cup white wine
- 2 cups cooked white or brown rice

****Jalapeño and serrano peppers can sting and irritate the skin, so wear rubber gloves when handling peppers and do not touch your eyes.***

1. Heat 2 tablespoons oil in large skillet over medium heat. Add sausage; cook about 10 minutes or until browned. Transfer to paper towel-lined plate with slotted spoon.

2. Heat remaining 2 tablespoons oil in same skillet. Add flour; cook until dark brown but not burnt, whisking constantly. Add chicken, onions, celery, bell peppers, jalapeño peppers and paprika. Cook and stir 7 to 8 minutes or until vegetables soften. Transfer to **CROCK-POT®** slow cooker.

3. Add sausage, okra, broth and wine to **CROCK-POT®** slow cooker. Cover; cook on LOW 7 to 8 hours or on HIGH 4 to 6 hours. Serve over rice.

Makes 6 servings

Mushroom-Beef Stew

- 1 pound beef stew meat
- 1 can (10 3/4 ounces) condensed cream of mushroom soup, undiluted
- 2 cans (4 ounces each) sliced mushrooms, drained
- 1 package (1 ounce) dry onion soup mix
- Hot cooked egg noodles

Combine all ingredients except noodles in **CROCK-POT®** slow cooker. Cover; cook on LOW 8 to 10 hours. Serve over noodles.

Makes 4 servings

Note: Button mushrooms are the most common mushrooms grown and sold. They are plump and dome-shaped with a smooth texture and mild flavor. The color of button mushrooms varies from white to pale tan.

Mrs. Grady's Beans

- **1/2 pound ground beef**
- **1 onion, chopped**
- **8 slices bacon, chopped**
- **1 can (about 15 ounces) pinto beans, undrained**
- **1 can (about 15 ounces) butter beans, rinsed and drained, reserving 1/4 cup liquid**
- **1 can (about 15 ounces) kidney beans, rinsed and drained**
- **1/4 cup ketchup**
- **2 tablespoons molasses**
- **1/2 teaspoon dry mustard**
- **1/2 cup granulated sugar**
- **1/4 cup packed brown sugar**

1. Brown ground beef, onion and bacon in medium saucepan over high heat. Stir in beans and liquid; set aside.

2. Combine ketchup, molasses and mustard in medium bowl. Mix in granulated sugar and brown sugars. Stir ketchup mixture into beef mixture; mix well. Transfer to **CROCK-POT®** slow cooker. Cover; cook on LOW 2 to 3 hours or until heated through.

Makes 6 to 8 servings

Roast Chicken with Peas, Prosciutto and Cream 

- **1 whole chicken (about $2\frac{1}{2}$ pounds), cut up**
- **Salt and black pepper**
- **5 ounces prosciutto, diced**
- **1 white onion, finely chopped**
- **½ cup dry white wine**
- **1 package (10 ounces) frozen peas**
- **½ cup whipping cream**
- **1½ tablespoons cornstarch**
- **2 tablespoons water**
- **4 cups farfalle pasta, cooked and drained**

1. Season chicken with salt and pepper. Combine chicken, prosciutto, onion and wine in **CROCK-POT®** slow cooker. Cover; cook on LOW 8 to 10 hours or on HIGH 4 to 5 hours.

2. During last 30 minutes of cooking, add peas and cream to cooking liquid.

3. Remove chicken. Remove meat from bones and set aside on a warmed platter.

4. Combine cornstarch and water in small bowl. Add to cooking liquid in **CROCK-POT®** slow cooker. Turn **CROCK-POT®** slow cooker to HIGH. Cover; cook on HIGH 10 to 15 minutes or until thickened.

5. Spoon pasta onto individual plates. Place chicken on pasta and top each portion with sauce.

Makes 6 servings

No-Fuss Macaroni & Cheese

- 2 cups (about 8 ounces) uncooked elbow macaroni
- 4 ounces light pasteurized process cheese, cubed
- 1 cup (4 ounces) shredded mild Cheddar cheese
- 1/2 teaspoon salt
- 1/8 teaspoon black pepper
- 1 1/2 cups fat-free (skim) milk

Combine macaroni, cheeses, salt and pepper in **CROCK-POT®** slow cooker. Pour milk over all. Cover; cook on LOW 2 to 3 hours, stirring after 20 to 30 minutes.

Makes 6 to 8 servings

Old-Fashioned Split Pea Soup

- **4 quarts chicken broth**
- **2 pounds dried split peas**
- **1 cup chopped ham**
- **½ cup chopped onion**
- **½ cup chopped celery**
- **2 teaspoons salt**
- **2 teaspoons black pepper**

1. Combine all ingredients in **CROCK-POT®** slow cooker. Cover; cook on LOW 8 to 10 hours or on HIGH 4 to 6 hours, or until peas are soft.

2. Using a hand mixer or hand blender, purée soup until smooth.

Makes 8 servings

Rustic Cheddar Mashed Potatoes

- **2 pounds russet potatoes, peeled and diced**
- **1 cup water**
- **1/3 cup butter, cut into small pieces**
- **1/2 to 3/4 cup milk**
- **1 1/4 teaspoons salt**
- **1/2 teaspoon black pepper**
- **1/2 cup finely chopped green onions**
- **1/2 to 3/4 cup (2 to 3 ounces) shredded Cheddar cheese**

1. Combine potatoes and water in **CROCK-POT®** slow cooker; dot with butter. Cover; cook on LOW 6 hours or on HIGH 3 hours, or until potatoes are tender. Transfer potatoes to large bowl.

2. Beat potatoes with electric mixer at medium speed until well blended. Add milk, salt and pepper; beat until well blended.

3. Stir in green onions and cheese; cover. Let stand 15 minutes or until cheese is melted.

Makes 8 servings

Chicken and Black Bean Chili

- 1 pound boneless, skinless chicken thighs, cut into 1-inch pieces
- 2 teaspoons chili powder
- 2 teaspoons ground cumin
- 3/4 teaspoon salt
- 1 green bell pepper, diced
- 1 onion, chopped
- 3 cloves garlic, minced
- 1 can (about 14 ounces) diced tomatoes
- 1 cup chunky salsa
- 1 can (about 15 ounces) black beans, rinsed and drained

Toppings: sour cream, diced ripe avocado, shredded Cheddar cheese, sliced green onions or chopped cilantro, crushed tortilla chips or corn chips

1. Combine chicken, chili powder, cumin and salt in **CROCK-POT®** slow cooker, tossing to coat.

2. Add bell pepper, onion and garlic; mix well. Stir in tomatoes with juice and salsa. Cover; cook on LOW 5 to 6 hours or on HIGH 2½ to 3 hours, or until chicken is tender.

3. Turn **CROCK-POT®** slow cooker to HIGH; stir in beans. Cover; cook 5 to 10 minutes or until beans are heated through. Serve with desired toppings.

Makes 4 servings

Turkey Piccata

- $2\frac{1}{2}$ tablespoons all-purpose flour
- $\frac{1}{4}$ teaspoon salt
- $\frac{1}{4}$ teaspoon black pepper
- 1 pound turkey breast, cut into short strips*
- 1 tablespoon butter
- 1 tablespoon olive oil
- $\frac{1}{2}$ cup chicken broth
- 2 teaspoons freshly squeezed lemon juice
- Grated peel of 1 lemon
- 2 cups cooked rice (optional)
- 2 tablespoons finely chopped parsley

You may substitute turkey tenderloins; cut as directed.

1. Combine flour, salt and pepper in large resealable food storage bag. Add turkey and shake well to coat. Heat butter and oil in large skillet over medium-high heat. Add turkey in single layer; brown on all sides, about 2 minutes per side. Transfer to **CROCK-POT®** slow cooker, arranging on bottom in single layer.

2. Pour broth into skillet. Cook and stir to scrape up any browned bits. Pour into **CROCK-POT®** slow cooker. Add lemon juice and peel. Cover; cook on LOW 1 hour. Serve over rice, if desired. Sprinkle with parsley before serving.

Makes 4 servings

Tip: This recipe will also work with chicken strips. Start with boneless, skinless chicken breasts, then follow the recipe as directed.

Nana's Beef Brisket

- 1 onion, thinly sliced
- 1 beef brisket (2 to 2½ pounds)
- ½ teaspoon salt
- ½ teaspoon black pepper
- ⅔ cup chili sauce, divided
- 1½ tablespoons packed brown sugar
- ¼ teaspoon ground cinnamon
- 2 sweet potatoes, peeled and cut into 1-inch pieces
- 1 cup (5 ounces) pitted prunes
- 2 tablespoons cornstarch
- 2 tablespoons cold water

1. Place onion in **CROCK-POT®** slow cooker. Arrange brisket over onion (tucking edges under to fit, if necessary). Sprinkle with salt and pepper; top with ⅓ cup chili sauce. Cover; cook on HIGH 3½ hours.

2. Combine remaining ⅓ cup chili sauce, brown sugar and cinnamon in large bowl. Add sweet potatoes and prunes; toss to coat. Spoon mixture over brisket. Cover; cook on HIGH 1¼ to 1½ hours or until brisket and sweet potatoes are tender.

3. Transfer brisket to cutting board; tent with foil. Transfer sweet potato mixture to serving platter with slotted spoon. Keep warm.

4. Blend cornstarch into water in small cup until smooth. Stir mixture into cooking liquid. Cover; cook on HIGH 10 minutes or until sauce is thickened.

5. Cut brisket crosswise into thin slices. Serve with sweet potato mixture and sauce.

Makes 8 servings

Pizza Soup

- **2 cans (about 14 ounces each) stewed tomatoes with Italian seasonings, undrained**
- **2 cups beef broth**
- **1 cup sliced mushrooms**
- **1 onion, chopped**
- **1 tablespoon tomato paste**
- **1/4 teaspoon salt**
- **1/4 teaspoon black pepper**
- **1/2 pound turkey Italian sausage, casings removed**
- **Shredded mozzarella cheese**

1. Combine tomatoes with juice, broth, mushrooms, onion, tomato paste, salt and pepper in **CROCK-POT®** slow cooker.

2. Shape sausage into marble-size balls. Gently stir into soup mixture. Cover; cook on LOW 6 to 7 hours. Serve with cheese.

Makes 4 servings

Gratin Potatoes with Asiago Cheese

- **6 slices bacon, cut into 1-inch pieces**
- **6 baking potatoes, peeled and thinly sliced**
- **1/2 cup grated Asiago cheese**
- **Salt and black pepper**
- **1 1/2 cups whipping cream**

1. Heat skillet over medium heat. Add bacon; cook and stir until crispy. Transfer to paper towel-lined plate with slotted spoon.

2. Transfer bacon fat to **CROCK-POT®** slow cooker. Layer one-fourth of potatoes on bottom of **CROCK-POT®** slow cooker. Sprinkle one fourth of bacon over potatoes and top with one fourth of cheese. Add salt and pepper. Repeat layers three times. Pour cream over all. Cover; cook on LOW 7 to 9 hours or on HIGH 5 to 6 hours.

Makes 4 to 6 servings

Pork Tenderloin with Cabbage

- 3 cups shredded red cabbage
- 1/4 cup chopped onion
- 1/4 cup chicken broth or water
- 1 clove garlic, minced
- 1 1/2 pounds pork tenderloin
- 3/4 cup apple juice concentrate
- 3 tablespoons honey mustard
- 1 1/2 tablespoons Worcestershire sauce

1. Place cabbage, onion, broth and garlic in **CROCK-POT®** slow cooker. Place pork over cabbage mixture. Combine apple juice concentrate, mustard and Worcestershire sauce in small bowl. Pour over pork. Cover and cook on LOW 6 to 8 hours or on HIGH 3 to 4 hours.

2. Slice pork and serve with cabbage and juices.

Makes 6 servings

Potato Cheddar Soup

- 2 pounds new red potatoes, peeled and cut into 1/2-inch cubes
- 3/4 cup coarsely chopped carrots
- 1 onion, coarsely chopped
- 1/2 teaspoon salt
- 3 cups chicken broth
- 1 cup half-and-half
- 1/4 teaspoon black pepper
- 2 cups (about 8 ounces) shredded Cheddar cheese

1. Place potatoes, carrots, onion and salt in **CROCK-POT®** slow cooker. Pour in broth. Cover; cook on LOW 6 to 7 hours or on HIGH 3 to 3½ hours, or until vegetables are tender.

2. Turn **CROCK-POT®** slow cooker to HIGH. Stir in half-and-half and pepper. Cover; cook on HIGH 15 minutes. Turn off heat. Uncover; let stand 5 minutes. Add cheese; stir until melted.

Makes 6 servings

Serving Suggestion: Try this soup topped with whole wheat croutons.

Family Get-Togethers

Knockwurst and Cabbage

- Olive oil
- 8 to 10 knockwurst sausage links
- 1 head red cabbage, cut into $1/4$-inch slices
- $1/2$ cup thinly sliced white onion
- 2 teaspoons caraway seeds
- 1 teaspoon salt
- 4 cups chicken broth

1. Heat oil in large skillet over medium heat. Brown sausages on all sides. Transfer to **CROCK-POT®** slow cooker.

2. Add cabbage and onion to **CROCK-POT®** slow cooker. Sprinkle with caraway seeds and salt. Add broth. Cover; cook on LOW 4 hours or on HIGH about 2 hours, or until sausages are cooked through and cabbage and onion are soft.

Makes 8 servings

Sausage, Butter Beans and Cabbage Soup

- 2 tablespoons butter, divided
- 1 onion, chopped
- 12 ounces smoked sausage such as kielbasa or andouille, cut into 1/2-inch slices
- 8 cups chicken broth
- 1/2 head savoy cabbage, coarsely shredded
- 3 tablespoons tomato paste
- 1 bay leaf
- 4 medium tomatoes, chopped
- 2 cans (about 14 ounces each) butter beans, drained
- Salt and black pepper

1. Melt 1 tablespoon butter in large skillet over medium heat. Add onion; cook and stir 3 to 4 minutes or until golden. Place in **CROCK-POT®** slow cooker.

2. Melt remaining 1 tablespoon butter in same skillet. Add sausage; cook and stir until brown. Add to **CROCK-POT®** slow cooker.

3. Place broth, cabbage, tomato paste and bay leaf in **CROCK-POT®** slow cooker; stir until well blended. Cover; cook on LOW 4 hours or on HIGH 2 hours.

4. Add tomatoes and beans; season with salt and pepper. Cover; cook on LOW 1 hour until heated through. Remove and discard bay leaf.

Makes 6 servings

Tip: Savoy cabbage is an excellent cooking cabbage with a full head of crinkled leaves varying from dark to pale green. Green cabbage may be substituted.

Mama's Best Baked Beans

- 1 bag (1 pound) dried Great Northern beans
- 1 package (1 pound) bacon
- 5 hot dogs, cut into 1/2-inch pieces
- 1 cup chopped onion
- 1 bottle (24 ounces) ketchup
- 2 cups packed dark brown sugar

1. Soak and cook beans according to package directions. Drain and refrigerate until ready to use.

2. Cook bacon in large skillet over medium-high heat until crisp. Drain on paper towels. Crumble bacon; set aside. Discard all but 3 tablespoons bacon fat from skillet. Add hot dogs and onion. Cook and stir over medium heat until onion is tender.

3. Combine cooked beans, bacon, hot dog mixture, ketchup and brown sugar in **CROCK-POT®** slow cooker. Cover; cook on LOW 2 to 4 hours.

Makes 4 to 6 servings

Happy Holidays

Ham with Fruited Bourbon Sauce

- 1 bone-in ham, butt portion (about 6 pounds)
- 3/4 cup packed dark brown sugar
- 1/2 cup apple juice
- 1/2 cup raisins
- 1 teaspoon ground cinnamon
- 1/4 teaspoon red pepper flakes
- 1/3 cup dried cherries
- 1/4 cup cornstarch
- 1/4 cup bourbon, rum or apple juice

1. Coat **CROCK-POT®** slow cooker with nonstick cooking spray. Add ham, cut side up. Combine brown sugar, apple juice, raisins, cinnamon and red pepper flakes in small bowl; stir well. Pour mixture evenly over ham. Cover; cook on LOW 9 to 10 hours or on HIGH 4½ to 5 hours. Add cherries 30 minutes before end of cooking time.

2. Transfer ham to cutting board. Let stand 15 minutes before slicing.

3. Pour cooking liquid into large measuring cup and let stand 5 minutes. Skim and discard excess fat. Return cooking liquid to **CROCK-POT®** slow cooker.

4. Turn **CROCK-POT®** slow cooker to HIGH. Whisk cornstarch and bourbon in small bowl until cornstarch is dissolved. Stir into cooking liquid. Cover; cook on HIGH 15 to 20 minutes or until thickened. Serve sauce over sliced ham.

Makes 10 to 12 servings

Corn Bread Stuffing with Sausage and Green Apples

- **1 package (16 ounces) honey corn bread mix, plus ingredients to prepare mix**
- **2 cups cubed French bread**
- **1½ pounds mild Italian sausage, casings removed**
- **1 onion, finely chopped**
- **1 green apple, peeled, cored and diced**
- **2 stalks celery, finely chopped**
- **¼ teaspoon dried sage**
- **¼ teaspoon dried rosemary**
- **¼ teaspoon dried thyme**
- **½ teaspoon salt**
- **¼ teaspoon black pepper**
- **3 cups chicken broth**
- **2 tablespoons fresh chopped parsley (optional)**

1. Mix and bake corn bread according to package directions. When cool, cover with plastic wrap and set aside overnight.*

2. Coat **CROCK-POT®** slow cooker with nonstick cooking spray. Preheat oven to 350°F. Cut corn bread into 1-inch cubes. Spread corn bread and French bread on baking sheet. Toast in oven about 20 minutes or until dry.

3. Meanwhile, heat medium skillet over medium heat. Add sausage; cook and stir until browned. Transfer sausage to **CROCK-POT®** slow cooker with slotted spoon.

4. Add onion, apple and celery to skillet. Cook and stir 5 minutes or until softened. Stir in sage, rosemary, thyme, salt and pepper. Transfer mixture to **CROCK-POT®** slow cooker.

5. Add bread cubes and stir gently to combine. Pour broth over mixture. Cover; cook on HIGH 3 to 3½ hours or until liquid is absorbed. Garnish with parsley.

Makes 8 to 12 servings

Or purchase prepared 8-inch square pan of corn bread. Proceed as directed.

Buttery Vegetable Gratin

- **3 leeks, halved lengthwise, cut into 1-inch pieces**
- **1 red bell pepper, cut into 1/2-inch pieces**
- **5 tablespoons unsalted butter, divided**
- **1/4 cup grated Parmesan cheese, divided**
- **1 teaspoon fresh thyme, divided**
- **3/4 teaspoon salt, divided**
- **1/4 plus 1/8 teaspoon black pepper, divided**
- **2 zucchini (about 1 1/2 pounds total), cut into 3/4-inch-thick slices**
- **2 yellow squash (about 1 1/2 pounds total), cut into 3/4-inch-thick slices**
- **1 1/2 cups fresh bread crumbs**

1. Generously grease **CROCK-POT®** slow cooker. Sprinkle leeks and bell pepper over bottom of **CROCK-POT®** slow cooker. Dot with 1 tablespoon butter, 1 tablespoon cheese, 1/2 teaspoon thyme, 1/4 teaspoon salt and 1/8 teaspoon black pepper.

2. Arrange zucchini in a single layer over leeks, overlapping as necessary. Dot with 1 tablespoon butter, 1 tablespoon cheese, remaining 1/2 teaspoon thyme, 1/4 teaspoon salt and 1/8 teaspoon black pepper.

3. Arrange yellow squash in a single layer over zucchini, overlapping as necessary. Dot with 1 tablespoon butter, remaining 2 tablespoons cheese, 1/4 teaspoon salt and 1/8 teaspoon black pepper. Cover; cook on LOW 4 to 5 hours or until vegetables are soft.

4. Meanwhile, melt remaining 2 tablespoons butter in large nonstick skillet over medium-high heat. Add bread crumbs; cook and stir 6 minutes or until crisp and golden brown. Transfer to a bowl and cool. Sprinkle over vegetable mixture just before serving.

Makes 12 servings

Beef Stew with Molasses and Raisins

- 1/3 cup all-purpose flour
- 2 teaspoons salt, divided
- 1 1/2 teaspoons black pepper, divided
- 2 pounds beef stew meat, cut into 1 1/2-inch pieces
- 5 tablespoons oil, divided
- 2 onions, sliced
- 1 can (about 28 ounces) diced tomatoes, drained
- 1 cup beef broth
- 3 tablespoons molasses
- 2 tablespoons cider vinegar
- 4 cloves garlic, minced
- 2 teaspoons dried thyme
- 1 teaspoon celery salt
- 1 bay leaf
- 8 ounces baby carrots, cut in half lengthwise
- 2 parsnips, diced
- 1/2 cup golden raisins

1. Combine flour, 1 1/2 teaspoons salt and 1 teaspoon pepper in large bowl. Toss beef in flour mixture. Heat 2 tablespoons oil in large skillet or Dutch oven over medium-high heat. Add half of beef and brown on all sides. Set aside browned beef and repeat with 2 additional tablespoons oil and remaining beef.

2. Add remaining 1 tablespoon oil to skillet. Add onions and cook 5 minutes, stirring to scrape up browned bits. Add tomatoes, broth, molasses, vinegar, garlic, thyme, celery salt, bay leaf and remaining 1/2 teaspoon salt and 1/2 teaspoon pepper. Bring to a boil. Add browned beef and boil 1 minute.

3. Transfer mixture to **CROCK-POT®** slow cooker. Cover; cook on LOW 5 hours or on HIGH 2 1/2 hours. Add carrots, parsnips and raisins. Cover; cook 1 to 2 hours or until vegetables are tender. Remove and discard bay leaf before serving.

Makes 6 to 8 servings

Sweet Potato & Pecan Casserole

- 1 can (40 ounces) sweet potatoes, drained and mashed
- 1/2 cup apple juice
- 1/3 cup plus 2 tablespoons butter, melted, divided
- 1/2 teaspoon salt
- 1/2 teaspoon ground cinnamon
- 1/4 teaspoon black pepper
- 2 eggs
- 1/3 cup chopped pecans
- 1/3 cup packed brown sugar
- 2 tablespoons all-purpose flour

1. Combine sweet potatoes, apple juice, 1/3 cup butter, salt, cinnamon and pepper in large bowl. Beat in eggs. Place mixture in **CROCK-POT®** slow cooker.

2. Combine pecans, brown sugar, flour and remaining 2 tablespoons butter in small bowl. Spread over sweet potatoes in **CROCK-POT®** slow cooker. Cover; cook on HIGH 3 to 4 hours.

Makes 6 to 8 servings

Roast Ham with Tangy Mustard Glaze

- 1 fully cooked boneless ham (about 3 pounds), visible fat removed
- 1/4 cup packed dark brown sugar
- 2 tablespoons lemon juice, divided
- 1 tablespoon Dijon mustard
- 1/2 teaspoon ground allspice
- 1/4 cup granulated sugar
- 2 tablespoons cornstarch

1. Place ham in **CROCK-POT®** slow cooker. Combine brown sugar, 2 teaspoons lemon juice, mustard and allspice. Spoon evenly over ham. Cover; cook on LOW 6 to 7 hours or until ham is warm throughout and sauce is well absorbed. Transfer ham to warm serving platter.

2. Pour cooking liquid from **CROCK-POT®** slow cooker into small heavy saucepan. Add remaining lemon juice, granulated sugar and cornstarch. Cook over medium-high heat until mixture boils. Reduce to medium heat. Cook and stir until sauce is thickened and glossy.

3. Carve ham into slices and spoon sauce over individual servings.

Makes 12 to 15 servings

Spiced Beer Fondue

- 2 tablespoons butter
- 2 tablespoons all-purpose flour
- 1/2 cup half-and-half
- 1 cup light-colored beer, such as ale or lager
- 1 cup (about 4 ounces) shredded smoked gouda cheese
- 2 teaspoons coarse grain mustard
- 1 teaspoon Worcestershire sauce
- 1/8 teaspoon salt
- 1/8 teaspoon ground red pepper
- Dash ground nutmeg (optional)
- Apple slices, bread cubes, cooked potato pieces and chopped vegetables

1. Melt butter in medium saucepan over medium heat. Sprinkle with flour. Stir with whisk until smooth. Whisk in half-and-half and beer. Bring to a boil and cook 2 minutes, whisking constantly. Gradually stir in cheese, mustard, Worcestershire sauce, salt and red pepper. Cook and stir until cheese is completely melted and fondue is bubbly and smooth.

2. Coat **CROCK-POT® LITTLE DIPPER®** slow cooker with nonstick cooking spray. Fill with warm fondue. Sprinkle with nutmeg, if desired, and serve with apple slices, bread cubes, potato pieces and vegetables.

Makes 1 1/2 cups

Autumn Herbed Chicken with Fennel and Squash

- 3 to 4 pounds chicken thighs
- Salt and black pepper
- All-purpose flour
- 2 tablespoons olive oil
- 1 fennel bulb, thinly sliced
- ½ butternut squash, peeled, seeded and cut into ¾-inch cubes
- 1 teaspoon dried thyme
- ¾ cup walnuts (optional)
- ¾ cup chicken broth
- ½ cup apple cider or juice
- Cooked rice or pasta
- ¼ cup fresh basil, sliced into ribbons
- 2 teaspoons fresh rosemary, finely minced

1. Season chicken on all sides with salt and pepper, then lightly coat with flour. Heat oil in skillet over medium heat. Brown chicken in batches 3 to 5 minutes on each side. Remove with slotted spoon. Transfer to **CROCK-POT®** slow cooker.

2. Add fennel, squash and thyme. Stir well to combine. Add walnuts, if desired, broth and cider. Cover; cook on LOW 5 to 7 hours or on HIGH 2½ to 4½ hours.

3. Serve over rice or pasta and garnish with basil and rosemary.

Makes 6 servings

Brussels Sprouts with Bacon, Thyme and Raisins

- 2 pounds Brussels sprouts
- 1 cup chicken broth
- 2/3 cup golden raisins
- 2 thick slices applewood smoked bacon, chopped
- 2 tablespoons chopped fresh thyme

Trim ends from sprouts; cut in half lengthwise through core (or in quarters if large). Combine all ingredients in **CROCK-POT®** slow cooker. Cover; cook on LOW 3 to 4 hours.

Makes 8 servings

Green Bean Casserole

- 2 packages (10 ounces each) frozen green beans, thawed
- 1 can ($10^3/_4$ ounces) condensed cream of mushroom soup, undiluted
- 1 tablespoon chopped fresh parsley
- 1 tablespoon chopped roasted red peppers
- 1 teaspoon dried sage
- 1/2 teaspoon salt
- 1/2 teaspoon black pepper
- 1/4 teaspoon ground nutmeg
- 1/2 cup toasted slivered almonds

Combine all ingredients except almonds in **CROCK-POT®** slow cooker. Cover; cook on LOW 3 to 4 hours. Sprinkle with almonds before serving.

Makes 4 to 6 servings

Seared Pork Roast with Currant Cherry Salsa 

- 1½ teaspoons chili powder
- ¾ teaspoon salt
- ½ teaspoon garlic powder
- ½ teaspoon paprika
- ¼ teaspoon ground allspice
- 1 boneless pork loin roast (2 pounds)
- ½ cup water
- 1 pound bag frozen pitted dark cherries, thawed, drained and halved
- ¼ cup currants or dark raisins
- 1 teaspoon balsamic vinegar
- 1 teaspoon grated orange peel
- ⅛ to ¼ teaspoon red pepper flakes

1. Combine chili powder, salt, garlic powder, paprika and allspice in small bowl. Coat roast evenly with spice mixture, pressing spices into roast.

2. Coat large skillet with nonstick cooking spray; heat over medium-high heat. Brown roast on all sides. Place in **CROCK-POT®** slow cooker.

3. Pour water into skillet, stirring to scrape up browned bits. Pour liquid into **CROCK-POT®** slow cooker around roast. Cover; cook on LOW 6 to 8 hours.

4. Remove roast from **CROCK-POT®** slow cooker. Tent with foil; keep warm. Strain juices from **CROCK-POT®** slow cooker; discard solids. Pour juices into small saucepan; keep warm over low heat.

5. Add cherries, currants, vinegar, orange peel and red pepper flakes to **CROCK-POT®** slow cooker. Turn **CROCK-POT®** slow cooker to HIGH. Cover; cook on HIGH 30 minutes. Slice pork and spoon warm juices over meat. Serve with salsa.

Makes 8 servings

Horseradish Roast Beef and Potatoes

- 1 tablespoon freshly grated horseradish
- 1 tablespoon Dijon mustard
- 1 tablespoon minced fresh parsley
- 1 teaspoon thyme, basil or oregano
- 3 pounds beef roast
- 1 to 2 pounds Yukon Gold potatoes, peeled and quartered
- 1 pound mushrooms, cut into large chunks
- 2 cans (10½ ounces each) beef consommé
- 2 tomatoes, seeded and diced
- 1 onion, sliced
- 1 green bell pepper, chopped
- 1 red bell pepper, chopped
- 1 cup red wine
- 3 cloves garlic, minced
- 1 bay leaf
- Salt and black pepper

1. Combine horseradish, Dijon mustard, parsley and thyme in small bowl to make paste. Place roast in **CROCK-POT®** slow cooker and spread paste over roast.

2. Add remaining ingredients to **CROCK-POT®** slow cooker. Add enough water to cover roast and vegetables. Cover; cook on HIGH 2 hours. Turn **CROCK-POT®** slow cooker to LOW and cook 4 to 6 hours or until roast and vegetables are tender. Remove and discard bay leaf before serving.

Makes 12 servings

Harvest Ham Supper

- 6 carrots, cut into 2-inch pieces
- 3 sweet potatoes, quartered
- 1 to $1^1/_2$ pounds boneless ham
- 1 cup maple syrup

1. Arrange carrots and potatoes in bottom of **CROCK-POT®** slow cooker to form rack.

2. Place ham on top of vegetables. Pour syrup over ham and vegetables. Cover; cook on LOW 6 to 8 hours.

Makes 6 servings

Beef with Apples and Sweet Potatoes

- 1 boneless beef chuck shoulder roast (about 2 pounds), cut into 2-inch pieces
- 1 can (40 ounces) sweet potatoes, drained
- 2 onions, sliced
- 2 apples, cored and sliced
- 1/2 cup beef broth
- 2 cloves garlic, minced
- 1 teaspoon salt
- 1 teaspoon dried thyme, divided
- 3/4 teaspoon black pepper, divided
- 1 tablespoon cornstarch
- 1/4 teaspoon ground cinnamon
- 2 tablespoons cold water

1. Place beef, potatoes, onions, apples, broth, garlic, salt, 1/2 teaspoon thyme and 1/2 teaspoon pepper in **CROCK-POT®** slow cooker. Cover; cook on LOW 8 to 9 hours.

2. Transfer beef, potatoes, onions and apples to platter; cover with foil to keep warm. Let cooking liquid stand 5 minutes to allow fat to rise. Skim off fat and discard.

3. Stir together cornstarch, remaining 1/2 teaspoon thyme, 1/4 teaspoon pepper, cinnamon and water in small bowl until smooth; stir into cooking liquid. Turn **CROCK-POT®** slow cooker to HIGH. Cook 15 minutes or until cooking liquid is thickened. Serve sauce over beef, potatoes, onions and apples.

Makes 6 servings

Tip: Because **CROCK-POT®** slow cookers cook at a low heat for a long time, they're a great way to cook dishes calling for less-tender cuts of meat, since long, slow cooking helps tenderize these cuts.

Molasses Maple Glazed Beef Brisket

- 1 tablespoon salt
- 1 teaspoon ground red pepper
- 1/2 teaspoon black pepper
- 1 beef brisket (1 1/2 to 2 pounds), scored with a knife on both sides
- 1/2 cup maple syrup
- Juice of 1 orange
- 1/4 cup molasses
- 2 tablespoons packed light brown sugar
- 2 tablespoons olive oil
- 1 tablespoon tomato paste
- 2 cloves garlic, mashed
- 4 thin slices fresh ginger
- 4 thin slices orange peel, avoiding bitter white pith

1. Combine salt, red pepper and black pepper in small bowl. Rub mixture over brisket. Place brisket in large resealable bag.

2. Combine maple syrup, orange juice, molasses, brown sugar, oil, tomato paste, garlic, ginger and orange peel in small bowl. Pour mixture over brisket.

3. Refrigerate brisket 2 hours or overnight, turning bag several times.

4. Transfer brisket to **CROCK-POT®** slow cooker. Cover; cook on LOW 7 to 9 hours or on HIGH 3 1/2 to 4 hours, turning once or twice. Slice thinly across grain to serve.

Makes 4 to 6 servings

Braised Beets with Cranberries

- 2½ pounds medium beets, peeled and cut into 6 pieces
- ½ cup sweetened dried cranberries
- 2 tablespoons honey
- 2 tablespoons butter, cut into small pieces
- 2 tablespoons quick-cooking tapioca
- ½ teaspoon salt
- 1 cup cranberry juice
- ⅓ cup crumbled blue cheese (optional)
- Orange peel, thinly sliced or grated (optional)

1. Combine beets, cranberries, honey, butter, tapioca, salt and cranberry juice in **CROCK-POT®** slow cooker. Cover; cook on LOW 7 to 8 hours or until beets are tender.

2. Transfer beets to serving bowl with slotted spoon. Pour half of cooking liquid over beets. Serve warm, at room temperature, or chilled and sprinkled with blue cheese and orange peel, if desired.

Makes 6 to 8 servings

Winter Squash and Apples

- 1 teaspoon salt
- 1/2 teaspoon black pepper
- 1 butternut squash (about 2 pounds), peeled, seeded and cut into 2-inch pieces
- 2 apples, cored and cut into slices
- 1 medium onion, quartered and sliced
- 1 1/2 tablespoons butter

1. Combine salt and pepper in small bowl; set aside.

2. Place squash, apples and onion in **CROCK-POT®** slow cooker. Sprinkle with salt mixture; stir well. Cover; cook on LOW 6 to 7 hours or until vegetables are tender.

3. Just before serving, stir in butter and season to taste with additional salt and pepper.

Makes 4 to 6 servings

Pumpkin Bread Pudding

- 2 cups whole milk
- ½ cup plus 2 tablespoons butter, divided
- 1 cup solid-pack pumpkin
- 3 eggs
- 1 cup packed dark brown sugar, divided
- 1 tablespoon ground cinnamon
- 2 teaspoons vanilla
- ½ teaspoon ground nutmeg
- ¼ teaspoon salt
- 16 slices cinnamon raisin bread, torn into small pieces (8 cups total)
- ½ cup whipping cream
- 2 tablespoons bourbon (optional)

1. Coat inside of **CROCK-POT®** slow cooker with nonstick cooking spray.

2. Combine milk and 2 tablespoons butter in medium microwavable bowl. Microwave on HIGH 2½ to 3 minutes or until very hot.

3. Whisk pumpkin, eggs, ½ cup brown sugar, cinnamon, vanilla, nutmeg and salt in large bowl until well blended. Whisk in milk mixture until blended. Add bread cubes; toss to coat.

4. Transfer to **CROCK-POT®** slow cooker. Cover; cook on HIGH 2 hours or until knife inserted into center comes out clean. Turn off heat. Uncover; let stand 15 minutes.

5. Combine remaining ½ cup butter, ½ cup brown sugar and cream in a small saucepan. Bring to a boil over high heat, stirring frequently. Remove from heat. Stir in bourbon, if desired. Spoon bread pudding into individual bowls and top with sauce.

Makes 8 servings

Pumpkin-Cranberry Custard

1 can (30 ounces) pumpkin pie filling

1 can (12 ounces) evaporated milk

1 cup dried cranberries

4 eggs, beaten

1 cup crushed or whole gingersnap cookies (optional)

Whipped cream (optional)

Combine pumpkin, evaporated milk, cranberries and eggs in **CROCK-POT®** slow cooker; mix thoroughly. Cover; cook on HIGH 4 to 4½ hours. Serve with crushed or whole gingersnaps and whipped cream, if desired.

Makes 4 to 6 servings

Cran-Cherry Bread Pudding

- 3 egg yolks, beaten
- 1½ cups light cream
- ⅓ cup sugar
- ¼ teaspoon kosher salt
- 1½ teaspoons cherry extract
- ⅔ cup dried sweetened cranberries
- ⅔ cup golden raisins
- ½ cup whole candied red cherries, halved
- ¾ cup sherry
- 9 cups unseasoned stuffing mix or 18 slices bread, dried in the oven and cut into ½-inch cubes
- 1 cup white chocolate baking chips
- Whipped cream

1. Place three 18×3-inch strips of heavy-duty foil (or regular foil folded to double thickness) in **CROCK-POT®** slow cooker, crisscrossing to form spokes across bottom and up sides. Grease 2-quart baking dish.

2. Cook and stir egg yolks, cream, sugar and salt in medium heavy saucepan over medium heat until mixture coats back of spoon. Remove from heat. Set saucepan in sink of ice water and stir to cool. Stir in cherry extract. Transfer to bowl; press plastic wrap onto surface of custard; refrigerate.

3. Combine cranberries, raisins and cherries in small bowl. Heat sherry until warm. Pour over fruit; set aside for 10 minutes.

4. Fold bread cubes and baking chips into custard. Drain fruit, reserving sherry, and stir into batter. Pour into prepared dish. Top with reserved sherry and cover tightly with foil. Place on foil handles in **CROCK-POT®** slow cooker. Add 1 inch water to **CROCK-POT®** slow cooker. Cover; cook on LOW 3½ to 5½ hours or until pudding springs back when touched. Carefully remove dish using foil handles. Uncover; let stand 10 minutes. Serve warm with whipped cream.

Makes 12 servings

Cinnamon Latté

- 6 cups double-strength brewed coffee*
- 2 cups half-and-half
- 1 cup sugar
- 1 teaspoon vanilla
- 3 cinnamon sticks, plus additional for garnish
- Whipped cream (optional)

Double the amount of coffee grounds normally used to brew coffee. Or substitute 8 teaspoons instant coffee dissolved in 6 cups boiling water.

1. Blend coffee, half-and-half, sugar and vanilla in 3- to 4-quart **CROCK-POT®** slow cooker. Add 3 cinnamon sticks. Cover; cook on HIGH 3 hours.

2. Remove cinnamon sticks. Serve latté in tall coffee mugs with additional cinnamon sticks and whipped cream, if desired.

Makes 6 to 8 servings

Mocha Supreme

2 quarts strong brewed coffee
½ cup instant hot chocolate beverage mix
1 cinnamon stick, broken in half
1 cup whipping cream
1 tablespoon powdered sugar

1. Place coffee, hot chocolate mix and cinnamon stick halves in **CROCK-POT®** slow cooker; stir. Cover; cook on HIGH 2 to 2½ hours.

2. Remove and discard cinnamon stick halves.

3. Beat cream in medium bowl with electric mixer on high speed until soft peaks form. Add powdered sugar; beat until stiff peaks form. Ladle coffee mixture into mugs; top with whipped cream.

Makes 8 servings

Tip: To whip cream more quickly, chill the beaters and bowl in the freezer for 15 minutes.

Make It and Take It

Asian Pork Tenderloin

1/2 cup bottled garlic ginger sauce
1/4 cup sliced green onions
1 pork tenderloin (about 1 pound)
1 red onion, cut into chunks
1 red bell pepper, cut into 1-inch pieces
1 zucchini, cut into 1/4-inch slices
1 tablespoon olive oil

1. Place ginger sauce and green onions in large resealable food storage bag. Add pork; seal bag and turn to coat evenly. Refrigerate 30 minutes or overnight.

2. Combine red onion, bell pepper, zucchini and oil in large bowl; toss to coat. Place vegetables in **CROCK-POT®** slow cooker. Remove pork from bag and place on top of vegetables. Discard marinade. Cover; cook on LOW 6 to 7 hours or on HIGH 4 to 5 hours.

3. Remove pork to cutting board; cover loosely with foil and let stand 10 minutes before slicing. Serve pork with vegetables.

Makes 4 servings

Polenta Lasagna

- **4 cups boiling water**
- **1½ cups whole grain yellow cornmeal**
- **4 teaspoons finely chopped fresh marjoram**
- **1 teaspoon olive oil**
- **1 pound mushrooms, sliced**
- **1 cup chopped leeks**
- **1 clove garlic, minced**
- **½ cup (2 ounces) shredded part-skim mozzarella cheese**
- **2 tablespoons chopped fresh basil**
- **1 tablespoon chopped fresh oregano**
- **⅛ teaspoon black pepper**
- **2 red bell peppers, chopped**
- **¼ cup water**
- **¼ cup freshly grated Parmesan cheese, divided**

1. Coat **CROCK-POT®** slow cooker with nonstick cooking spray. Combine boiling water and cornmeal in **CROCK-POT®** slow cooker; mixing well. Stir in marjoram. Cover; cook on LOW 3 to 4 hours or on HIGH 1 to 2 hours, stirring occasionally. Cover and chill about 1 hour or until firm.

2. Heat oil in medium nonstick skillet over medium heat. Cook and stir mushrooms, leeks and garlic 5 minutes or until leeks are crisp-tender. Stir in mozzarella, basil, oregano and black pepper.

3. Place bell peppers and ¼ cup water in food processor or blender; cover and process until smooth.

4. Cut cold polenta in half and place one half in bottom of **CROCK-POT®** slow cooker. Top with half of bell pepper mixture, half of vegetable mixture and 2 tablespoons Parmesan. Place remaining polenta over Parmesan; top with remaining bell pepper and vegetable mixtures and Parmesan. Cover; cook on LOW 3 hours or until Parmesan cheese is melted and polenta is golden brown.

Makes 6 servings

Lemon-Mint Red Potatoes

- **2 pounds new red potatoes**
- **3 tablespoons extra virgin olive oil**
- **1 teaspoon salt**
- **3/4 teaspoon dried Greek seasoning or dried oregano**
- **1/4 teaspoon garlic powder**
- **1/4 teaspoon black pepper**
- **1/4 cup chopped fresh mint, divided**
- **2 tablespoons butter**
- **2 tablespoons lemon juice**
- **1 teaspoon grated lemon peel**

1. Coat inside of **CROCK-POT®** slow cooker with nonstick cooking spray. Add potatoes and oil, stirring gently to coat. Sprinkle with salt, Greek seasoning, garlic powder and pepper. Cover and cook on LOW 7 hours or on HIGH 4 hours.

2. Stir in 2 tablespoons mint, butter, lemon juice and lemon peel. Stir until butter is completely melted. Cover and cook 15 minutes to allow flavors to blend. Sprinkle with remaining mint.

Makes 4 servings

Tip: It's easy to prepare these potatoes ahead of time. Simply follow the recipe and then turn off the heat. Let it stand at room temperature for up to 2 hours. You may reheat or serve the potatoes at room temperature.

Beans with Smoky Canadian Bacon

- 2 cans (about 14 ounces each) diced fire-roasted tomatoes, undrained
- 1 can (about 15 ounces) pinto beans, rinsed and drained
- 1 package (8 ounces) Canadian bacon, cut into 1/2-inch cubes
- 1/2 cup Texas-style barbecue sauce*
- 1 onion, finely chopped
- 1/2 teaspoon salt
- 1/8 teaspoon crushed red pepper flakes (optional)
- Black pepper

***Look for barbecue sauce with liquid smoke as an ingredient.**

Combine all ingredients in **CROCK-POT®** slow cooker. Cover; cook on LOW 5 to 7 hours. Serve in bowls.

Makes 4 servings

Orange and Brown Sugar Whipped Butternut Squash

- 2 packages (20 ounces each) peeled, cubed butternut squash
- 1/2 cup chicken broth
- 3 tablespoons packed light brown sugar
- 2 tablespoons unsalted butter
- 1 teaspoon grated orange peel
- 3/4 teaspoon salt

Generously grease **CROCK-POT®** slow cooker. Add squash, broth, brown sugar and butter. Cover; cook on LOW 3 hours or until squash cubes are very tender. Drain and discard liquid. Transfer to food processor; process until smooth. Return to **CROCK-POT®** slow cooker; stir in orange peel and salt. Turn **CROCK-POT®** slow cooker to HIGH. Cover; cook 10 minutes.

Makes 7 to 8 servings

Beans with Smoky
Canadian Bacon

Fudge and Cream Pudding Cake

- **2 tablespoons unsalted butter**
- **1 cup all-purpose flour**
- **3/4 cup packed light brown sugar**
- **5 tablespoons unsweetened cocoa powder, divided**
- **2 teaspoons baking powder**
- **1/2 teaspoon ground cinnamon**
- **1/8 teaspoon salt**
- **1 cup light cream**
- **1 tablespoon vegetable oil**
- **1 teaspoon vanilla**
- **3/4 cup packed dark brown sugar**
- **1 3/4 cups hot water**
- **Whipped cream or ice cream (optional)**

1. Grease 4 1/2-quart **CROCK-POT®** slow cooker with butter. Combine flour, light brown sugar, 3 tablespoons cocoa, baking powder, cinnamon and salt in medium bowl. Add cream, oil and vanilla; stir well to combine. Pour batter into **CROCK-POT®** slow cooker.

2. Combine dark brown sugar and remaining 2 tablespoons cocoa in medium bowl. Add hot water; stir well to combine. Pour sauce over cake batter. Do not stir. Cover; cook on HIGH 2 hours.

3. Spoon onto plates. Serve with whipped cream, if desired.

Makes 8 to 10 servings

Pork Meatballs in Garlicky Almond Sauce

- ½ cup blanched whole almonds
- 1 cup chicken broth
- ⅓ cup roasted red pepper
- 4 teaspoons minced garlic, divided
- 1 teaspoon salt, divided
- ½ teaspoon saffron threads (optional)
- 1 cup fresh bread crumbs, divided
- ¼ cup dry white wine or chicken broth
- 1 pound ground pork
- ¼ cup finely chopped onion
- 1 egg, lightly beaten
- 3 tablespoons minced fresh parsley

1. Place almonds in food processor; process until finely ground. Add broth, red pepper, 2 teaspoons garlic, ½ teaspoon salt and saffron, if desired; process until smooth. Stir in ¼ cup bread crumbs. Transfer to **CROCK-POT®** slow cooker.

2. Place remaining ¾ cup bread crumbs in large bowl; sprinkle with wine and stir gently. Add pork, onion, egg, parsley, remaining 2 teaspoons garlic and ½ teaspoon salt; mix well. Shape into 24 (1-inch) balls.

3. Coat a large skillet with nonstick cooking spray and heat over medium-high heat. Cook meatballs in batches, turning to brown on all sides. Transfer to **CROCK-POT®** slow cooker with sauce as batches are done. Cover; cook on HIGH 3 to 4 hours or until meatballs are cooked through.

Makes 6 servings

Provençal Lemon and Olive Chicken

- 2 cups chopped onion
- 8 skinless chicken thighs (about 2½ pounds)
- 1 lemon, thinly sliced and seeds removed
- 1 cup pitted green olives
- 1 tablespoon olive brine from jar or white vinegar
- 2 teaspoons herbes de Provence
- 1 bay leaf
- ½ teaspoon salt
- ⅛ teaspoon black pepper
- 1 cup chicken broth
- ½ cup minced fresh parsley

1. Place onion in **CROCK-POT®** slow cooker. Arrange chicken over onion. Place lemon slice on each thigh. Add olives, brine, herbes de Provence, bay leaf, salt and pepper. Slowly pour in broth.

2. Cover; cook on LOW 5 to 6 hours or on HIGH 3 to 3½ hours or until chicken is tender. Remove and discard bay leaf. Stir in parsley before serving.

Makes 8 servings

Note: To skin chicken easily, grasp skin with paper towel and pull away. Repeat with fresh paper towel for each piece of chicken, discarding skins and towels.

Mushroom and Romano Risotto

- 3 tablespoons extra virgin olive oil
- 8 ounces sliced mushrooms
- 1/2 cup chopped shallots
- 1/2 cup chopped onion
- 3 cloves garlic, minced
- 1 1/2 cups arborio rice
- 1/2 cup Madeira wine
- 4 1/2 cups vegetable broth
- 1/2 cup Romano cheese
- 3 tablespoons unsalted butter
- 3 tablespoons chopped fresh parsley
- 1/4 teaspoon black pepper

1. Heat oil in large nonstick skillet over medium-high heat. Add mushrooms; cook and stir 6 to 7 minutes or until mushrooms begin to brown. Stir in shallots, onion and garlic; cook and stir 2 to 3 minutes or until vegetables begin to soften. Add rice; cook and stir 1 minute. Add wine; cook and stir 1 minute or until almost absorbed.

2. Transfer mixture to **CROCK-POT®** slow cooker. Add broth. Cover; cook on HIGH 2 hours or until liquid is absorbed and rice is tender.

3. Turn off heat and stir in cheese, butter, parsley and pepper. Serve immediately.

Makes 4 servings

Old-Fashioned Sauerkraut

- 8 slices bacon, chopped
- 2 pounds sauerkraut
- 1 large head cabbage or 2 small heads cabbage
- 2½ cups chopped onions
- ¼ cup (½ stick) butter
- 2 tablespoons sugar
- 1 teaspoon salt
- 1 teaspoon black pepper

1. Heat large skillet over medium heat. Cook and stir bacon until crisp. Remove skillet from heat and set aside. (Do not drain bacon fat.)

2. Place sauerkraut, cabbage, onions, butter, sugar, salt and pepper in **CROCK-POT®** slow cooker. Pour bacon and bacon fat over sauerkraut mixture. Cover; cook on LOW 4 to 5 hours or on HIGH 1 to 3 hours.

Makes 8 to 10 servings

Note: Serve with your favorite bratwurst, knockwurst or other sausage.

Cheesy Broccoli Casserole

- 2 packages (10 ounces each) frozen chopped broccoli, thawed
- 1 can ($10^3/_4$ ounces) condensed cream of celery soup, undiluted
- $1^1/_4$ cups shredded sharp Cheddar cheese, divided
- $^1/_4$ cup minced onion
- $^1/_2$ teaspoon celery seeds
- 1 teaspoon paprika
- 1 teaspoon hot pepper sauce
- 1 cup crushed potato chips or saltine crackers

1. Coat **CROCK-POT®** slow cooker with nonstick cooking spray. Combine broccoli, soup, 1 cup cheese, onion, celery seeds, paprika and hot pepper sauce in **CROCK-POT®** slow cooker; mix well. Cover; cook on LOW 5 to 6 hours or on HIGH $2^1/_2$ to 3 hours.

2. Uncover; sprinkle top with potato chips and remaining $^1/_4$ cup cheese. Cook, uncovered, on LOW 30 to 60 minutes or on HIGH 15 to 30 minutes, or until cheese is melted.

Makes 4 to 6 servings

Tip: For a change in taste, prepare with thawed chopped spinach instead of broccoli, and top with crushed crackers or spicy croutons to complement the cheesy crust.

Mushroom Wild Rice

- 1 cup uncooked wild rice (or wild rice and rice mixture)
- 1/2 cup sliced mushrooms
- 1/2 cup diced onion
- 1/2 cup diced red or green bell pepper
- 1 1/2 cups chicken broth
- 1 tablespoon olive oil
- 1/4 teaspoon salt
- 1/4 teaspoon black pepper

Layer rice, mushrooms, onion and bell pepper in **CROCK-POT®** slow cooker. Add broth, oil, salt and black pepper. Cover; cook on HIGH 2½ hours or until rice is tender and liquid is absorbed.

Makes 8 servings

Chorizo and Corn Bread Dressing

- **½ pound chorizo sausage, removed from casings***
- **1 can (about 14 ounces) chicken broth**
- **1 can (10¾ ounces) condensed cream of chicken soup, undiluted**
- **1 box (6 ounces) corn bread stuffing mix**
- **1 cup chopped onion**
- **1 cup diced red bell pepper**
- **1 cup chopped celery**
- **1 cup frozen corn**
- **3 eggs, lightly beaten**

A highly seasoned Mexican pork sausage.

1. Coat **CROCK-POT®** slow cooker with nonstick cooking spray.

2. Brown chorizo 6 to 8 minutes in large skillet over medium-high heat, stirring to break up meat. Transfer to **CROCK-POT®** slow cooker with slotted spoon.

3. Stir broth and chicken soup into skillet. Add remaining ingredients and stir until well blended. Stir into **CROCK-POT®** slow cooker. Cover and cook on LOW 7 hours or on HIGH 3½ hours.

Makes 4 to 6 servings

Mexican-Style Rice and Cheese

- **1 can (about 15 ounces) Mexican-style beans, rinsed and drained**
- **1 can (about 14 ounces) diced tomatoes with chiles**
- **2 cups (8 ounces) shredded Monterey Jack or Colby cheese, divided**
- **1½ cups uncooked converted long grain rice**
- **1 onion, finely chopped**
- **½ (8-ounce) package cream cheese**
- **3 cloves garlic, minced**

1. Coat **CROCK-POT®** slow cooker with nonstick cooking spray. Combine beans, tomatoes, 1 cup Monterey Jack cheese, rice, onion, cream cheese and garlic in **CROCK-POT®** slow cooker; mix well.

2. Cover; cook on LOW 6 to 8 hours or until rice is tender.

3. Sprinkle with remaining 1 cup Monterey Jack cheese just before serving.

Makes 6 to 8 servings

New England Baked Beans

- 4 slices uncooked bacon, chopped
- 3 cans (about 15 ounces each) Great Northern beans, rinsed and drained
- 3/4 cup water
- 1 onion, chopped
- 1/3 cup canned diced tomatoes, well drained
- 3 tablespoons packed light brown sugar
- 3 tablespoons maple syrup
- 3 tablespoons unsulphured molasses
- 2 cloves garlic, minced
- 1/2 teaspoon salt
- 1/2 teaspoon dry mustard
- 1/8 teaspoon black pepper
- 1/2 bay leaf

1. Cook bacon in large skillet until almost cooked but not crispy. Drain on paper towels.

2. Combine bacon and remaining ingredients in **CROCK-POT®** slow cooker. Cover; cook on LOW 6 to 8 hours or until mixture is thickened. Remove and discard bay leaf before serving.

Makes 4 to 6 servings

Cheesy Corn and Peppers

- 2 pounds frozen corn
- 2 poblano chile peppers, chopped, or 1 large green bell pepper and 1 jalapeño, seeded and finely chopped*
- 2 tablespoons butter, cut into cubes
- 1 teaspoon salt
- 1/2 teaspoon ground cumin
- 1/4 teaspoon coarsely ground black pepper
- 3 ounces cream cheese, cut into cubes
- 1 cup (4 ounces) shredded sharp Cheddar cheese

****Poblano and jalapeño peppers can sting and irritate the skin, so wear rubber gloves when handling peppers and do not touch your eyes.***

1. Coat **CROCK-POT®** slow cooker with nonstick cooking spray. Combine all ingredients except cream cheese and Cheddar cheese in **CROCK-POT®** slow cooker. Cover; cook on HIGH 2 hours.

2. Stir in cheeses. Cover; cook on HIGH 15 minutes or until cheeses are melted.

Makes 8 servings

Chicken Sausage Pilaf

- 1 pound uncooked chicken or turkey sausage, casings removed
- 1 package (about 7 ounces) uncooked chicken rice and vermicelli pasta mix
- 4 cups chicken broth
- 2 stalks celery, sliced
- 1/4 cup slivered almonds
- Salt and black pepper

1. Brown sausage in large skillet over medium-high heat, stirring to break up meat. Drain fat. Add rice and pasta mix to skillet. Cook and stir 1 minute. Transfer to **CROCK-POT®** slow cooker.

2. Add broth, celery, almonds, salt and pepper to **CROCK-POT®** slow cooker; mix well.

3. Cover; cook on LOW 7 to 10 hours or on HIGH 3 to 4 hours, or until rice is tender.

Makes 4 servings

Creamy Red Pepper Polenta

- **1/4 cup (1/2 stick) butter, melted**
- **1/4 teaspoon paprika, plus additional for garnish**
- **1/8 teaspoon ground red pepper**
- **1/8 teaspoon ground cumin**
- **6 cups boiling water**
- **2 cups yellow cornmeal**
- **1 red bell pepper, finely chopped**
- **2 teaspoons salt**

Combine butter, 1/4 teaspoon paprika, red pepper and cumin in **CROCK-POT®** slow cooker. Add boiling water, cornmeal, bell pepper and salt. Stir well to combine. Cover; cook on LOW 3 to 4 hours or on HIGH 1 to 2 hours, stirring occasionally. Garnish with additional paprika.

Makes 4 to 6 servings

Spinach Spoon Bread

- 1 package (10 ounces) frozen chopped spinach, thawed and squeezed dry
- 1 red bell pepper, diced
- 1 package (5½ ounces) corn bread mix
- 4 eggs, lightly beaten
- 1 cup cottage cheese
- 6 green onions, sliced
- ½ cup (1 stick) butter, melted
- 1¼ teaspoons seasoned salt

1. Coat **CROCK-POT®** slow cooker with nonstick cooking spray. Preheat on HIGH.

2. Combine all ingredients in large bowl; mix well. Pour batter into prepared **CROCK-POT®** slow cooker. Cover; cook with lid slightly ajar to allow excess moisture to escape, on LOW 3 to 4 hours or on HIGH 1¾ to 2 hours, or until edges are golden and knife inserted into center comes out clean.

3. Loosen edges and bottom with knife and invert onto plate. Cut into wedges or spoon from **CROCK-POT®** slow cooker to serve.

Makes 8 servings

Mixed Berry Cobbler

- 1 package (16 ounces) frozen mixed berries
- 3/4 cup granulated sugar
- 2 tablespoons quick-cooking tapioca
- 2 teaspoons grated lemon peel
- 1 1/2 cups all-purpose flour
- 1/2 cup packed light brown sugar
- 2 1/4 teaspoons baking powder
- 1/4 teaspoon ground nutmeg
- 3/4 cup milk
- 1/3 cup butter, melted
- Vanilla ice cream or whipped cream (optional)

1. Coat **CROCK-POT®** slow cooker with nonstick cooking spray. Combine berries, granulated sugar, tapioca and lemon peel in medium bowl. Transfer to **CROCK-POT®** slow cooker.

2. Combine flour, brown sugar, baking powder and nutmeg in medium bowl. Add milk and butter; stir just until blended. Drop spoonfuls of dough on top of berry mixture. Cover; cook on LOW 4 hours. Uncover; let stand about 30 minutes. Serve with ice cream, if desired.

Makes 8 servings

Tip: Cobblers are year-round favorites. Experiment with seasonal fresh fruits, such as pears, plums, peaches, rhubarb, blueberries, raspberries, strawberries, blackberries or gooseberries. Or try different apple varieties, including newer ones such as Pink Lady, or a blend of your favorite apples to come up with your own signature cobbler.

Cherry Delight

- 1 can (21 ounces) cherry pie filling
- 1 package (about 18 ounces) yellow cake mix
- 1/2 cup (1 stick) butter, melted
- 1/3 cup chopped walnuts
- Whipped topping or vanilla ice cream (optional)

1. Place pie filling in **CROCK-POT®** slow cooker. Combine cake mix and butter in medium bowl. Spread evenly over pie filling. Sprinkle walnuts on top.

2. Cover; cook on LOW 3 to 4 hours or on HIGH 1½ to 2 hours. Spoon into serving dishes. Serve warm with whipped topping or ice cream, if desired.

Makes 8 to 10 servings

Triple Chocolate Fantasy

- **2 pounds white almond bark, broken into pieces**
- **1 bar (4 ounces) sweetened chocolate, broken into pieces***
- **1 package (12 ounces) semisweet chocolate chips**
- **3 cups lightly toasted, coarsely chopped pecans****

Use your favorite high-quality chocolate candy bar.

*****To toast pecans, spread in single layer in heavy-bottomed skillet. Cook over medium heat, stirring frequently, until pecans are lightly browned. Remove from skillet immediately. Cool before using.***

1. Place bark, sweetened chocolate and chocolate chips in **CROCK-POT®** slow cooker. Cover; cook on HIGH 1 hour. Do not stir.

2. Turn **CROCK-POT®** slow cooker to LOW. Continue cooking 1 hour, stirring every 15 minutes. Stir in pecans.

3. Drop mixture by tablespoonfuls onto baking sheet covered with waxed paper; let cool. Store in tightly covered container.

Makes 36 pieces

Variations: Here are a few ideas for other imaginative items to add in along with or instead of pecans: raisins, crushed peppermint candy, candy-coated baking bits, crushed toffee, peanuts or pistachios, chopped gum drops, chopped dried fruit, candied cherries, chopped marshmallows or sweetened coconut.

Suppers and Potlucks

Boneless Chicken Cacciatore

- 2 tablespoons olive oil
- 6 boneless, skinless chicken breasts, sliced in half horizontally
- 4 cups tomato-basil pasta sauce or marinara sauce
- 1 cup coarsely chopped yellow onion
- 1 cup coarsely chopped green bell pepper
- 1 can (6 ounces) sliced mushrooms
- 1/4 cup dry red wine (optional)
- 2 teaspoons minced garlic
- 2 teaspoons dried oregano, crushed
- 2 teaspoons dried thyme, crushed
- 2 teaspoons salt
- 2 teaspoons black pepper

1. Heat oil in large skillet over medium heat. Brown chicken on both sides. Drain and transfer to **CROCK-POT®** slow cooker.

2. Add remaining ingredients; stir well to combine. Cover; cook on LOW 5 to 7 hours or on HIGH 2 to 3 hours.

Makes 6 servings

Basil Chicken Merlot with Wild Mushrooms

- **3 tablespoons extra virgin olive oil, divided**
- **1 roasting chicken (about 3 pounds), skinned and cut into individual pieces**
- **1½ cups thickly sliced cremini mushrooms**
- **1 yellow onion, diced**
- **2 cloves garlic, minced**
- **1 cup chicken broth**
- **1 can (6 ounces) tomato paste**
- **⅓ cup Merlot or other dry red wine**
- **2 teaspoons sugar**
- **1 teaspoon ground oregano**
- **¼ teaspoon salt**
- **¼ teaspoon black pepper**
- **2 tablespoons minced fresh basil**
- **3 cups cooked ziti pasta, drained**
- **Grated Romano cheese (optional)**

1. Heat 1½ to 2 tablespoons oil in large skillet over medium heat. Brown half of chicken on each side about 3 to 5 minutes. Remove with slotted spoon and repeat with remaining chicken. Set aside.

2. Heat remaining oil in skillet and add mushrooms, onion and garlic. Cook and stir 7 to 8 minutes or until onion is soft. Transfer to **CROCK-POT®** slow cooker. Top with chicken.

3. Combine broth, tomato paste, wine, sugar, oregano, salt and pepper in medium bowl. Pour sauce over chicken. Cover; cook on LOW 7 to 9 hours or on HIGH 3 to 4 hours.

4. Stir in basil. Place pasta in large serving bowl or on platter. Top with chicken, mushrooms and sauce. Garnish with cheese.

Makes 4 to 6 servings

Wild Rice and Mushroom Casserole

- 2 tablespoons olive oil
- 1/2 red onion, finely diced
- 1 green bell pepper, finely diced
- 8 ounces mushrooms, thinly sliced
- 1 can (about 14 ounces) diced tomatoes, drained
- 2 cloves garlic, minced
- 1 teaspoon dried oregano
- 1 teaspoon paprika
- 2 tablespoons butter
- 2 tablespoons all-purpose flour
- 1 1/2 cups milk
- 8 ounces pepper jack, Cheddar or Swiss cheese, shredded
- 1 teaspoon salt
- 1/2 teaspoon black pepper
- 2 cups wild rice, cooked according to package instructions

1. Heat oil in large skillet over medium heat. Add onion, bell pepper and mushrooms. Cook and stir 5 to 6 minutes, until vegetables are soft. Add tomatoes, garlic, oregano and paprika; cook until heated through. Transfer to large bowl; let cool.

2. Melt butter in skillet over medium heat; whisk in flour. Cook and stir 4 to 5 minutes until smooth and golden. Whisk in milk. Bring to a boil. Whisk in cheese until melted; season with salt and black pepper.

3. Combine wild rice with sautéed vegetables. Fold in cheese sauce and mix gently.

4. Grease inside of **CROCK-POT®** slow cooker. Pour in wild rice mixture. Cover; cook on LOW 4 to 6 hours or on HIGH 2 to 3 hours.

Makes 4 to 6 servings

Fall-Apart Pork Roast with Mole

- **2/3 cup whole almonds**
- **2/3 cup raisins**
- **3 tablespoons vegetable oil, divided**
- **1/2 cup chopped onion**
- **4 cloves garlic, chopped**
- **2 3/4 pounds lean boneless pork shoulder roast**
- **1 can (about 14 ounces) diced fire-roasted tomatoes or diced tomatoes**
- **1 cup cubed bread, any variety**
- **1/2 cup chicken broth**
- **2 ounces Mexican chocolate, chopped**
- **2 tablespoons chipotle peppers in adobo sauce, chopped**
- **1 teaspoon salt**
- **Fresh cilantro, coarsely chopped (optional)**

1. Heat large skillet over medium-high heat. Add almonds and toast 3 to 4 minutes, stirring frequently, until fragrant. Add raisins. Cook and stir 1 to 2 minutes or until raisins begin to plump. Place half of almond mixture in large bowl. Reserve remaining half for garnish.

2. Heat 1 tablespoon oil in same skillet. Add onion and garlic; cook and stir 2 minutes or until softened. Add to almond mixture; set aside.

3. Heat remaining oil in same skillet. Add pork roast and brown on all sides, about 5 to 7 minutes. Transfer to **CROCK-POT®** slow cooker.

4. Add tomatoes with juice, bread, broth, chocolate, chipotle peppers and salt to almond mixture. Place in blender or food processor in batches; process until smooth. Pour sauce over pork in **CROCK-POT®** slow cooker. Cover; cook on LOW 7 to 8 hours or on HIGH 3 to 4 hours.

5. Remove pork from **CROCK-POT®** slow cooker. Whisk sauce until smooth; spoon over pork. Garnish with reserved almond mixture and chopped cilantro.

Makes 6 servings

Turkey Stroganoff

- **4 cups sliced mushrooms**
- **2 stalks celery, thinly sliced**
- **2 shallots or 1/2 onion, minced**
- **1 cup chicken broth**
- **1/2 teaspoon dried thyme**
- **1/4 teaspoon black pepper**
- **2 turkey tenderloins, turkey breasts or boneless, skinless chicken thighs (about 10 ounces each), cut into bite-size chunks**
- **1/2 cup sour cream**
- **1 tablespoon plus 1 teaspoon all-purpose flour**
- **1/4 teaspoon salt**
- **1 1/3 cups cooked wide egg noodles**

1. Coat large skillet with nonstick cooking spray. Add mushrooms, celery and shallots; cook and stir over medium heat 5 minutes or until mushrooms and shallots are tender. Spoon into **CROCK-POT®** slow cooker. Stir in broth, thyme and pepper. Stir in turkey. Cover; cook on LOW 5 to 6 hours.

2. Combine sour cream and flour in small bowl. Spoon 2 tablespoons liquid from **CROCK-POT®** slow cooker into bowl; stir well. Stir sour cream mixture into **CROCK-POT®** slow cooker. Cover; cook 10 minutes. Stir in salt. Serve noodles topped with turkey mixture.

Makes 4 servings

Five-Bean Casserole 

2 onions, chopped
8 ounces bacon, diced
2 cloves garlic, minced
1/2 cup packed brown sugar
1/2 cup cider vinegar
1 teaspoon salt
1 teaspoon dry mustard
1/4 teaspoon black pepper
2 cans (about 15 ounces each) kidney beans, rinsed and drained
1 can (about 15 ounces) chickpeas, rinsed and drained
1 can (about 15 ounces) butter beans, rinsed and drained
1 can (about 15 ounces) Great Northern or cannellini beans, rinsed and drained
1 can (about 15 ounces) baked beans
Chopped green onions (optional)

1. Cook and stir onions, bacon and garlic in large skillet over medium heat until onions are tender; drain. Stir in brown sugar, vinegar, salt, mustard and pepper. Simmer over low heat 15 minutes.

2. Combine all beans in **CROCK-POT®** slow cooker. Spoon onion mixture evenly over top. Cover; cook on LOW 6 to 8 hours or on HIGH 3 to 4 hours. Garnish with green onions.

Makes 16 servings

Greek Rice

- **2 tablespoons butter**
- **$1^3/_4$ cups uncooked converted long grain rice**
- **2 cans (about 14 ounces each) chicken broth**
- **1 teaspoon Greek seasoning**
- **1 teaspoon ground oregano**
- **1 cup pitted kalamata olives, drained and chopped**
- **$^3/_4$ cup chopped roasted red peppers**
- **Crumbled feta cheese (optional)**
- **Chopped fresh Italian parsley (optional)**

1. Melt butter in large nonstick skillet over medium-high heat. Add rice; cook and stir 4 minutes or until golden brown. Transfer to **CROCK-POT®** slow cooker. Stir in broth, Greek seasoning and oregano.

2. Cover; cook on LOW 4 hours or until liquid is absorbed and rice is tender. Stir in olives and roasted red peppers and cook 5 minutes more. Garnish with feta and Italian parsley.

Makes 6 to 8 servings

Asian Beef with Broccoli

- $1^1/_2$ pounds boneless beef chuck steak (about $1^1/_2$ inches thick), sliced into thin strips*
- 1 can ($10^1/_2$ ounces) condensed beef consommé, undiluted
- $^1/_2$ cup oyster sauce
- 2 tablespoons cornstarch
- 1 bag (16 ounces) fresh broccoli florets
- Hot cooked rice
- Sesame seeds (optional)

****To make slicing steak easier, place in freezer for 30 minutes to firm up.***

1. Place beef in **CROCK-POT®** slow cooker. Pour consommé and oyster sauce over beef. Cover; cook on HIGH 3 hours.

2. Combine cornstarch and 2 tablespoons cooking liquid in small bowl. Add to **CROCK-POT®** slow cooker. Stir well to combine. Cover; cook on HIGH 15 minutes or until thickened.

3. Poke holes in broccoli bag with fork. Microwave on HIGH 3 minutes. Empty bag into **CROCK-POT®** slow cooker. Gently toss beef and broccoli together. Serve over rice. Garnish with sesame seeds.

Makes 4 to 6 servings

Bacon-Molasses Baked Beans

- **1 pound dry small white Great Northern or navy beans**
- **1 onion, finely chopped**
- **1/2 pound bacon, finely chopped**
- **1/3 cup light molasses**
- **1/4 cup packed dark brown sugar**
- **2 teaspoons dry mustard**
- **1/4 teaspoon coarsely ground black pepper**
- **1 1/2 teaspoons salt**

1. Discard any stones and shriveled beans. Rinse beans with cold running water. Cover beans with 2 inches of water in large bowl. Cover; let stand at room temperature overnight. Drain and rinse.

2. Stir beans, onion, bacon, molasses, brown sugar, mustard and pepper together in **CROCK-POT®** slow cooker. Add enough water to cover with 1 inch of water.

3. Cover; cook on LOW 8 hours or until beans are tender and sauce is thickened. Stir in salt.

Makes 15 servings

Lemon Dilled Parsnips and Turnips

- 2 cups chicken broth
- 1/4 cup chopped green onions
- 1/4 cup dried dill
- 1/4 cup lemon juice
- 1 teaspoon minced garlic
- 4 turnips, peeled and cut into 1/2-inch pieces
- 3 parsnips, peeled and cut into 1/2-inch pieces
- 1/4 cup cornstarch
- 1/4 cup cold water

1. Combine broth, green onions, dill, lemon juice and garlic in **CROCK-POT®** slow cooker.

2. Add turnips and parsnips; stir. Cover; cook on LOW 3 to 4 hours or on HIGH 1 to 3 hours.

3. Turn **CROCK-POT®** slow cooker to HIGH. Dissolve cornstarch in water. Add to **CROCK-POT®** slow cooker. Stir well to combine. Cover; cook 15 minutes or until thickened.

Makes 8 to 10 servings

Autumn Chicken

- 1 can (14 ounces) whole artichoke hearts, drained
- 1 can (14 ounces) whole mushrooms, divided
- 12 boneless, skinless chicken breasts
- 1 jar (6½ ounces) marinated artichoke hearts, undrained
- ¾ cup white wine
- ½ cup balsamic vinaigrette
- Hot cooked egg noodles
- Paprika (optional)

Spread whole artichokes over bottom of **CROCK-POT®** slow cooker. Top with half of mushrooms. Layer chicken over mushrooms. Add marinated artichoke hearts with liquid. Add remaining mushrooms. Pour in wine and vinaigrette. Cover; cook on LOW 4 to 5 hours. Serve over noodles. Garnish with paprika.

Makes 10 to 12 servings

Mediterranean Chicken

- 1 tablespoon olive oil
- 2 pounds boneless, skinless chicken breasts
- 1 can (about 28 ounces) diced tomatoes
- 2 onions, chopped
- 1/2 cup dry sherry
- Juice of 2 lemons
- 6 teaspoons minced garlic
- 2 cinnamon sticks
- 1 bay leaf
- 1/2 teaspoon black pepper
- 1 pound cooked broad noodles
- 1/2 cup feta cheese

1. Heat oil in large skillet. Add the chicken and lightly brown.

2. Combine tomatoes with juice, onions, sherry, lemon juice, garlic, cinnamon sticks, bay leaf and pepper in **CROCK-POT®** slow cooker. Add chicken. Cover; cook on LOW 8 to 10 hours or on HIGH 4 to 5 hours.

3. Discard cinnamon sticks and bay leaf. Serve chicken and sauce over cooked noodles. Sprinkle with cheese just before serving.

Makes 6 servings

Slow-Cooked Succotash

- **2 teaspoons canola oil**
- **1 cup diced onion**
- **1 cup diced green bell pepper**
- **1 cup diced celery**
- **1 teaspoon paprika**
- **1½ cups frozen white or yellow corn**
- **1½ cups frozen lima beans**
- **1 cup canned diced tomatoes, undrained**
- **2 teaspoons dried parsley flakes *or* 1 tablespoon minced fresh parsley**
- **½ teaspoon salt**
- **½ teaspoon black pepper**

1. Heat oil in large skillet over medium heat. Add onion, bell pepper and celery. Cook and stir 5 minutes or until onion is translucent and bell pepper and celery are crisp-tender. Stir in paprika.

2. Combine onion mixture with remaining ingredients in **CROCK-POT®** slow cooker. Mix thoroughly. Cover; cook on LOW 6 to 8 hours or on HIGH 3 to 4 hours.

Makes 8 servings

Mexican Corn Bread Pudding

- 1 can (about 15 ounces) cream-style corn
- 2 eggs, beaten
- 1 can (4 ounces) diced mild green chiles
- 2 tablespoons vegetable oil
- 3/4 cup yellow cornmeal
- 2 tablespoons sugar
- 2 teaspoons baking powder
- 3/4 teaspoon salt
- 1/2 cup shredded Cheddar cheese

Coat 2-quart **CROCK-POT®** slow cooker with nonstick cooking spray. Combine corn, eggs, chiles, oil, cornmeal, sugar, baking powder and salt in medium bowl. Stir well to blend. Pour into **CROCK-POT®** slow cooker. Cover; cook on LOW 2 to 2½ hours or until center is set. Sprinkle cheese over top. Cover and let stand 5 minutes or until cheese is melted.

Makes 8 servings

Macaroni and Cheese

- 6 cups cooked elbow macaroni
- 2 tablespoons butter
- 4 cups evaporated milk
- 6 cups (24 ounces) shredded Cheddar cheese
- 2 teaspoons salt
- 1/2 teaspoon black pepper

Toss macaroni with butter in large bowl. Stir in evaporated milk, cheese, salt and pepper; place in **CROCK-POT®** slow cooker. Cover; cook on HIGH 2 to 3 hours.

Makes 6 to 8 servings

Tip: Make this mac 'n' cheese recipe more fun. Add some tasty mix-ins: diced green or red bell pepper, peas, hot dog slices, chopped tomato, browned ground beef or chopped onion. Be creative!

Spanish Paella-Style Rice

- **2 cans (about 14 ounces each) chicken broth**
- **1 1/2 cups uncooked converted long grain rice**
- **1 red bell pepper, diced**
- **1/3 cup dry white wine or water**
- **1/2 teaspoon saffron threads, crushed or 1/2 teaspoon ground turmeric**
- **1/8 teaspoon red pepper flakes**
- **1/2 cup frozen peas, thawed**
- **Salt**

1. Combine broth, rice, bell pepper, wine, saffron and red pepper flakes in **CROCK-POT®** slow cooker; mix well. Cover; cook on LOW 4 hours or until liquid is absorbed.

2. Stir in peas. Cover; cook 15 to 30 minutes or until peas are heated through. Season with salt.

Makes 6 servings

Tip: Paella can contain a variety of meats as well. For more authenticity—and to turn this dish into a delicious main course—add 1/2 cup cooked ham, chicken, chorizo sausage or seafood when you add the peas.

Chicken and Portobello Stroganoff

- **2½ pounds boneless, skinless chicken thighs**
- **1 pound baby portobello mushrooms, cleaned and sliced***
- **1 cup frozen whole onions, thawed**
- **1 can (10½ ounces) condensed French onion soup, undiluted**
- **⅓ cup dry sherry**
- **1 tablespoon chopped fresh thyme *or* ½ teaspoon dried thyme**
- **½ teaspoon black pepper**
- **½ teaspoon coarse salt**
- **¼ cup all-purpose flour**
- **2 tablespoons butter, softened**
- **1 cup sour cream**
- **Hot cooked egg noodles**
- **Chopped fresh thyme (optional)**

Look for baby portobellos in the produce section of your supermarket. Substitute an equal weight of any other fresh mushrooms.

1. Place chicken, mushrooms and onions in **CROCK-POT®** slow cooker. Combine soup, sherry, 1 tablespoon thyme, pepper and salt in medium bowl. Pour over chicken and vegetables. Cover; cook on LOW 6 to 7 hours.
2. Combine flour and butter in small bowl until smooth. Stir into cooking liquid in **CROCK-POT®** slow cooker; cook 15 minutes or until thickened.
3. Stir in sour cream. Cover; cook 15 minutes. Serve chicken mixture over egg noodles and sprinkle with additional thyme, if desired.

Makes 6 to 8 servings

Sesame Chicken

- 4 chicken legs, bone-in (or 4 thighs and 4 drumsticks)
- 4 chicken breasts, bone-in
- 1 cup rice flour
- 8 teaspoons sesame seeds
- Salt and black pepper
- Vegetable oil
- 1 cup chicken broth
- 1/2 cup chopped celery
- 1/4 cup chopped onion
- 1 teaspoon dried tarragon
- 1/4 cup cornstarch
- 1/4 cup water
- 1 1/2 cups sour cream

1. Cut through joints to separate thighs and drumsticks. Split breasts in half. Mix rice flour, sesame seeds, salt and pepper in medium bowl. Dip chicken pieces in mixture to coat.

2. Heat oil in skillet over medium heat. Brown chicken on all sides, turning as it browns. Transfer to paper towel-lined plate with slotted spoon to drain excess fat. Place in **CROCK-POT®** slow cooker.

3. Add broth, celery, onion and tarragon. Cover; cook on LOW 7 to 8 hours or on HIGH 3 to 4 hours.

4. Turn **CROCK-POT®** slow cooker to HIGH. Combine cornstarch and water in small bowl. Add sour cream. Mix well to combine. Add to **CROCK-POT®** slow cooker. Stir gently to combine. Cover; cook on HIGH 15 to 20 minutes or until thickened.

Makes 4 to 6 servings

Swiss Cheese Scalloped Potatoes

- 2 pounds baking potatoes, peeled and thinly sliced, divided
- 1/2 cup finely chopped yellow onion, divided
- 1/4 teaspoon salt, divided
- 1/4 teaspoon ground nutmeg, divided
- 2 tablespoons butter, cut into small pieces, divided
- 1/2 cup milk
- 2 tablespoons all-purpose flour
- 3 ounces Swiss cheese slices, torn into small pieces
- 1/4 cup finely chopped green onions (optional)

1. Layer half the potatoes, 1/4 cup onion, 1/8 teaspoon salt, 1/8 teaspoon nutmeg and 1 tablespoon butter in **CROCK-POT®** slow cooker. Repeat layers. Cover; cook on LOW 7 hours or on HIGH 4 hours.

2. Remove potatoes with slotted spoon to serving dish; cover with foil to keep warm.

3. Whisk milk and flour in small bowl until smooth. Stir mixture into cooking liquid. Add cheese; stir to combine. Turn **CROCK-POT®** slow cooker to HIGH. Cover; cook 10 minutes or until slightly thickened. Stir; pour cheese mixture over potatoes. Sprinkle with green onions, if desired.

Makes 5 to 6 servings

Tip: Don't add water to the **CROCK-POT®** slow cooker unless a recipe specifically says so. Foods don't lose much moisture during slow cooking, so follow recipe guidelines.

Cherry Rice Pudding

- **$1\frac{1}{2}$ cups milk**
- **1 cup hot cooked rice**
- **3 eggs, beaten**
- **$\frac{1}{2}$ cup sugar**
- **$\frac{1}{4}$ cup dried cherries**
- **$\frac{1}{2}$ teaspoon almond extract**
- **$\frac{1}{4}$ teaspoon salt**
- **Ground nutmeg (optional)**

1. Combine all ingredients except nutmeg in large bowl. Pour into greased $1\frac{1}{2}$-quart casserole dish. Cover dish with buttered aluminum foil, butter side down.

2. Place rack in **CROCK-POT®** slow cooker and pour in 1 cup water. Place casserole on rack. Cover; cook on LOW 4 to 5 hours.

3. Remove casserole from **CROCK-POT®** slow cooker. Let stand 15 minutes before serving. Garnish with nutmeg.

Makes 6 servings

Variation: Try substituting dried cranberries for the dried cherries or add 2 tablespoons of each for a delicious new dish.

Peach Cobbler

- **2 packages (16 ounces each) frozen peaches, thawed and drained**
- **3/4 cup plus 1 tablespoon sugar, divided**
- **2 teaspoons ground cinnamon, divided**
- **1/2 teaspoon ground nutmeg**
- **3/4 cup all-purpose flour**
- **6 tablespoons butter, cut into small pieces**
- **Whipped cream (optional)**

1. Combine peaches, 3/4 cup sugar, 1½ teaspoons cinnamon and nutmeg in medium bowl. Transfer to **CROCK-POT®** slow cooker.

2. Combine flour, remaining 1 tablespoon sugar and remaining 1/2 teaspoon cinnamon in small bowl. Cut in butter with pastry blender or two knives until mixture resembles coarse crumbs. Sprinkle over peach mixture. Cover; cook on HIGH 2 hours. Serve with whipped cream, if desired.

Makes 4 to 6 servings

Tip: To make cleanup easier when cooking sticky or sugary foods, coat the inside of the **CROCK-POT®** slow cooker with nonstick cooking spray before adding ingredients.

Spring Flings

Coconut Rice Pudding

- **2 cups water**
- **1 cup uncooked converted long grain rice**
- **1 tablespoon unsalted butter**
- **Pinch salt**
- **2 1/4 cups evaporated milk**
- **1 can (about 14 ounces) cream of coconut**
- **1/2 cup golden raisins**
- **3 egg yolks, beaten**
- **Grated peel of 2 limes**
- **1 teaspoon vanilla**
- **Toasted shredded coconut (optional)**

1. Place water, rice, butter and salt in medium saucepan. Bring to a boil over high heat, stirring frequently. Reduce heat to low. Cover; cook 10 to 12 minutes. Remove from heat. Let stand, covered, 5 minutes.

2. Meanwhile, coat **CROCK-POT®** slow cooker with nonstick cooking spray. Add evaporated milk, cream of coconut, raisins, egg yolks, lime peel and vanilla; mix well. Add rice; stir until blended.

3. Cover; cook on LOW 4 hours or on HIGH 2 hours. Stir every 30 minutes. Pudding will thicken as it cools. Garnish with toasted coconut.

Makes 6 servings

Strawberry Rhubarb Crisp

Fruit

- **4 cups sliced strawberries**
- **4 cups diced rhubarb (about 5 stalks), cut into 1/2-inch dice**
- **1 1/2 cups granulated sugar**
- **2 tablespoons lemon juice**
- **1 1/2 tablespoons cornstarch, plus water (optional)**

Topping

- **1 cup all-purpose flour**
- **1 cup old-fashioned oats**
- **1/2 cup granulated sugar**
- **1/2 cup packed brown sugar**
- **1/2 teaspoon ground ginger**
- **1/2 teaspoon ground nutmeg**
- **1/2 cup (1 stick) butter, cut into pieces**
- **1/2 cup sliced almonds, toasted***

To toast almonds, spread in single layer on baking sheet. Bake in preheated 350°F oven 8 to 10 minutes or until golden brown, stirring frequently.

1. Coat **CROCK-POT®** slow cooker with nonstick cooking spray. Place strawberries, rhubarb, 1 1/2 cups granulated sugar and lemon juice in **CROCK-POT®** slow cooker and mix well. Cover; cook on HIGH 1 1/2 hours or until fruit is tender.

2. If fruit is dry after cooking, add 2 tablespoons water. If fruit is runny, mix cornstarch with a little water and stir into liquid. Cover; cook an additional 15 minutes or until cooking liquid is thickened.

3. Preheat oven to 375°F. Combine flour, oats, sugars, ginger and nutmeg in medium bowl. Cut in butter using pastry blender or two knives until mixture resembles coarse crumbs. Stir in almonds.

4. Sprinkle topping onto fruit in **CROCK-POT®** slow cooker. Transfer stoneware to oven. Bake 15 to 20 minutes or until topping begins to brown.

Makes 8 servings

Apple-Cranberry Crêpes

- **1 large baking apple, such as Gala or Jonathan, peeled and cut into 6 wedges**
- **1 large tart apple, such as Granny Smith, peeled and cut into 6 wedges**
- **1/4 cup dried sweetened cranberries or cherries**
- **2 tablespoons lemon juice**
- **1/2 teaspoon plus 1/8 teaspoon ground cinnamon, divided**
- **1/8 teaspoon ground nutmeg**
- **1/8 teaspoon ground cloves or allspice**
- **1 tablespoon butter**
- **1/4 cup orange juice**
- **1 tablespoon sugar**
- **3/4 teaspoon cornstarch**
- **1/4 teaspoon almond extract**
- **4 prepared crêpes**
- **1 cup vanilla ice cream (optional)**

1. Coat **CROCK-POT®** slow cooker with cooking spray. Place apple wedges, cranberries, lemon juice, 1/2 teaspoon cinnamon, nutmeg and cloves in **CROCK-POT®** slow cooker; toss to coat. Cover; cook on LOW 2 hours. Stir butter into apple mixture just until melted.

2. Combine orange juice, sugar, cornstarch and almond extract in small bowl; stir until cornstarch dissolves. Stir into apple mixture; mix well. Turn **CROCK-POT®** slow cooker to HIGH; cover; cook 15 minutes to thicken sauce slightly.

3. Place 1 crêpe on each of 4 dessert plates. Spoon apple mixture evenly down center of each crêpe. Fold edges over; place crêpes, seam sides down, on plates. Sprinkle with remaining 1/8 teaspoon cinnamon.

4. Heat filled crêpes in microwave, if desired, according to directions on package. Serve with ice cream, if desired.

Makes 4 servings

Duck Confit and Mushroom Salad

- 1/2 pound bacon, diced
- 2 shallots, thinly sliced
- 8 ounces mushrooms such as shiitake, oyster, chanterelles or a combination
- Kosher salt and black pepper
- 1 tablespoon Dijon mustard
- 1 tablespoon sherry wine vinegar
- 3 tablespoons extra virgin olive oil
- Sugar
- 1 1/2 pounds frisée lettuce or mesclun lettuce mix
- 2 cups Duck Confit (recipe follows)

1. Cook bacon in large skillet over medium-low heat to desired doneness. Drain bacon on paper towels.

2. Add shallots to skillet; cook 2 minutes, stirring often. Add mushrooms, salt and pepper. Cook 5 minutes or until soft. Remove from heat.

3. Whisk mustard and vinegar in medium bowl. Whisking constantly, slowly pour in thin stream of oil until dressing thickens. Season to taste with salt, pepper and sugar.

4. Combine frisée, mushrooms, bacon and 2 cups Duck Confit in large bowl. Pour dressing over and toss to coat. Serve immediately.

Makes 4 servings

Duck Confit and Mushroom Salad

Duck Confit

- 1 tablespoon black peppercorns
- 1 teaspoon coriander seeds
- 1 teaspoon dried thyme
- 1/2 teaspoon freshly grated nutmeg
- 1/2 teaspoon ground ginger
- 1 whole clove
- 1 bay leaf
- 1 tablespoon kosher salt, divided
- 1 whole duck (3 to 4 pounds)

1. Preheat broiler. Place all ingredients except salt and duck in spice grinder; grind 15 seconds.

2. Sprinkle 1½ teaspoons salt and half of spice mixture over breast side of duck. Place breast side down in broilerproof dish with sides at least 1½ inches high. Season back of duck with remaining salt and spice mixture.

3. Place duck on broiler pan; broil 10 minutes or until spices are fragrant and skin is starting to brown. Roll duck onto its side; broil 10 minutes. Repeat with last two sides of duck.

4. Transfer duck to **CROCK-POT®** slow cooker. Cover; cook on LOW 6 to 7 hours or on HIGH 3½ hours or until tender.

Makes 6 servings

Mexican Hot Pot

- 1 tablespoon canola oil
- 1 onion, chopped
- 3 cloves garlic, minced
- 2 teaspoons red pepper flakes
- 2 teaspoons dried oregano
- 1 teaspoon ground cumin
- 1 can (about 28 ounces) whole tomatoes, drained and chopped
- 2 cups whole kernel corn
- 1 can (about 15 ounces) chickpeas, rinsed and drained
- 1 can (about 15 ounces) pinto beans, rinsed and drained
- 1 cup water
- Shredded iceberg lettuce

1. Heat oil in large nonstick skillet over medium-high heat. Add onion and garlic; cook and stir 5 minutes. Add red pepper flakes, oregano and cumin; mix well.

2. Transfer onion and garlic mixture to **CROCK-POT®** slow cooker. Stir in tomatoes, corn, chickpeas, beans and water. Cover; cook on LOW 7 to 8 hours or on HIGH 2 to 3 hours.

3. Top each serving with shredded lettuce.

Makes 6 servings

Saag Paneer

- 2 onions, finely chopped
- 8 cloves garlic, minced
- 1 teaspoon ground coriander
- 1 teaspoon ground cumin
- ½ teaspoon pumpkin pie spice
- ½ teaspoon cardamom
- ½ teaspoon salt
- 2 packages (10 ounces each) frozen chopped spinach, thawed and squeezed dry
- 2 packages (9 ounces each) frozen chopped creamed spinach, thawed
- 2 tablespoons butter
- 8 ounces paneer or firm tofu, cut into ½-inch cubes

1. Combine onions, garlic, coriander, cumin, pumpkin pie spice, cardamom and salt in **CROCK-POT®** slow cooker. Add spinach, creamed spinach and butter. Cover; cook on LOW 4½ to 5 hours or until onions are soft.

2. Add paneer; cover and cook 30 minutes or until paneer is heated through.

Makes 10 servings

Corned Beef and Cabbage

- 2 onions, thickly sliced
- 1 corned beef brisket (about 3 pounds) with seasoning packet
- 1 package (8 to 10 ounces) baby carrots
- 6 potatoes, peeled and cut into wedges
- 1 cup water
- 3 to 5 slices bacon
- 1 head green cabbage, cut into wedges

1. Place onion slices on bottom of **CROCK-POT®** slow cooker. Add corned beef with seasoning packet, carrots and potato wedges. Pour 1 cup water over. Cover; cook on LOW 10 hours.

2. During last 30 minutes of cooking, heat large saucepan over medium-high heat. Add bacon; cook and stir until bacon is crisp. Drain on paper towels. Cool; crumble bacon.

3. Place cabbage in saucepan with bacon drippings. Cover with water. Bring to a boil and cook 20 to 30 minutes or until cabbage is tender. Drain.

4. Serve corned beef with vegetables. Top with crumbled bacon.

Makes 6 servings

Lentils with Walnuts

- 1 cup brown lentils
- 1 small onion or large shallot, chopped
- 1 stalk celery, trimmed and chopped
- 1 carrot, chopped
- 1/4 teaspoon crushed dried thyme
- 3 cups chicken broth
- Salt and black pepper, to taste
- 1/4 cup chopped walnuts

1. Combine lentils, onion, celery, carrot, thyme and broth in **CROCK-POT®** slow cooker. Cover; cook on HIGH 3 hours. Do not overcook. (Lentils should absorb most or all of broth. Slightly tilt **CROCK-POT®** slow cooker to check.)

2. Season with salt and pepper. Spoon lentils into serving bowl and sprinkle with walnuts.

Makes 4 to 6 servings

Variation: If desired, top dish with 4 cooked bacon strips cut into bite-size pieces. To serve as a main dish, stir in 1 cup diced cooked ham.

Asparagus and Cheese

- 2 cups crushed saltine crackers
- 1 can ($10^3/_4$ ounces) condensed cream of asparagus soup, undiluted
- 1 can ($10^3/_4$ ounces) condensed cream of chicken soup, undiluted
- $^2/_3$ cup slivered almonds
- 4 ounces American cheese, cut into cubes
- 1 egg
- $1^1/_2$ pounds fresh asparagus, trimmed

Combine crackers, soups, almonds, cheese and egg in large bowl; stir well. Pour into **CROCK-POT®** slow cooker. Add asparagus, and stir to coat. Cover; cook on HIGH 3 to $3^1/_2$ hours or until asparagus is tender. Garnish as desired.

Makes 4 to 6 servings

Tip: Cooking times are guidelines. **CROCK-POT®** slow cookers, just like ovens, cook differently depending on a variety of factors. For example, cooking times will be longer at higher altitudes. You may need to slightly adjust cooking times for your **CROCK-POT®** slow cooker.

Spring Pea and Mint Broth Soup

- **8 cups water**
- **3 carrots, cut into chunks**
- **2 onions, coarsely chopped**
- **2 to 3 leeks, coarsely chopped**
- **2 stalks celery, cut into chunks**
- **1 bunch fresh mint**
- **3 to 4 cups fresh spring peas or 1 bag (32 ounces) frozen peas**
- **1 tablespoon fresh lemon juice**
- **Kosher salt and black pepper**
- **Creme fraîche or sour cream**

1. Combine water, carrots, onions, leeks, celery and mint in **CROCK-POT®** slow cooker. Cover; cook on HIGH 5 hours.

2. Strain broth and return to **CROCK-POT®** slow cooker. Discard solids. Add peas and lemon juice. Cover; cook on LOW 4 to 5 hours or on HIGH 2 to 3 hours.

3. Season with salt and pepper. Ladle soup into bowls and garnish with dollop of creme fraîche.

Makes 6 to 8 servings

Note: Whether using farmstand-fresh spring peas or frozen sweet peas, this soup is fun to make. The aroma of fresh mint that fills the house is reason enough to try it.

Easy Vegetarian Vegetable Bean Soup

- 3 cans (about 14 ounces each) vegetable broth
- 2 cups cubed unpeeled potatoes
- 2 cups sliced leeks, white part only (about 3 medium)
- 1 can (about 14 ounces) diced tomatoes, undrained
- 1 onion, chopped
- 1 cup chopped or shredded cabbage
- 1 cup sliced celery
- 1 cup sliced carrots
- 3 cloves garlic, chopped
- 1/8 teaspoon dried rosemary
- 1 can (about 15 ounces) white beans, drained
- Salt and black pepper

1. Combine broth, potatoes, leeks, tomatoes with juice, onion, cabbage, celery, carrots, garlic and rosemary in **CROCK-POT®** slow cooker. Cover; cook on LOW 8 hours.

2. Stir in beans and season with salt and pepper. Cover; cook on LOW 30 minutes or until beans are heated through.

Makes 10 servings

Orange-Spice Glazed Carrots

- **1 package (32 ounces) baby carrots**
- **½ cup packed light brown sugar**
- **½ cup orange juice**
- **3 tablespoons butter or margarine**
- **¾ teaspoon ground cinnamon**
- **¼ teaspoon ground nutmeg**
- **¼ cup cold water**
- **2 tablespoons cornstarch**

1. Combine carrots, brown sugar, orange juice, butter, cinnamon and nutmeg in **CROCK-POT®** slow cooker. Cover; cook on LOW 3½ to 4 hours or until carrots are crisp-tender.

2. Spoon carrots into serving bowl. Transfer cooking liquid to small saucepan. Bring to a boil.

3. Mix water and cornstarch until smooth; stir into saucepan. Boil 1 minute or until thickened, stirring constantly. Spoon over carrots.

Makes 6 servings

Scallop and Corn Chowder

- **6 tablespoons butter, divided**
- **1 bunch leeks, cleaned well and diced**
- **3/4 pound pancetta, diced**
- **5 Yukon Gold potatoes, diced**
- **5 1/4 cups fish stock**
- **2 cups corn**
- **1 tablespoon minced fresh thyme, plus additional for garnish**
- **1/4 cup all-purpose flour**
- **1 pound sea scallops, quartered**
- **1 pint whipping cream**
- **Black pepper**

1. Heat 2 tablespoons butter in skillet over medium-high heat. Add leeks; cook and stir until softened and just beginning to brown. Transfer to **CROCK-POT®** slow cooker.

2. Cook pancetta until lightly browned in same skillet over medium heat; transfer to **CROCK-POT®** slow cooker. Add potatoes, stock, corn and 1 tablespoon thyme. Cover; cook on LOW 4 to 6 hours or on HIGH 2 to 3 hours, or until potatoes are tender.

3. Combine remaining 4 tablespoons butter and flour in large saucepan over medium heat. Cook and stir to make a thick, golden brown paste. Stir in 1 cup cooking liquid from **CROCK-POT®** slow cooker. Stir until well blended and return mixture to **CROCK-POT®** slow cooker. Add scallops and cook 10 minutes or until scallops are just cooked through.

4. Stir in cream. Garnish with pepper and additional thyme.

Makes 6 to 8 servings

Pesto Rice and Beans

- **1 can (about 15 ounces) Great Northern beans, rinsed and drained**
- **1 can (about 14 ounces) chicken broth**
- **3/4 cup uncooked converted long grain rice**
- **1 1/2 cups frozen cut green beans, thawed and drained**
- **1/2 cup prepared pesto**
- **Grated Parmesan cheese (optional)**

1. Combine Great Northern beans, broth and rice in **CROCK-POT®** slow cooker. Cover; cook on LOW 2 hours.

2. Stir in green beans. Cover; cook 1 hour or until rice and beans are tender.

3. Remove stoneware to heatproof surface. Stir in pesto and cheese, if desired. Cover; let stand 5 minutes or until cheese is melted. Serve immediately.

Makes 8 servings

Tip: Choose converted long grain rice (or Arborio rice when suggested) or wild rice for best results. Long, slow cooking can turn other types of rice into mush; if you prefer to use another type of rice instead of converted rice, cook it on the stove-top and add it to the **CROCK-POT®** slow cooker during the last 15 minutes of cooking.

Pineapple Rice Pudding

- 1 can (20 ounces) crushed pineapple in juice, undrained
- 1 can (about 14 ounces) coconut milk
- 1 can (12 ounces) evaporated milk
- 3/4 cup uncooked Arborio rice
- 2 eggs, lightly beaten
- 1/4 cup granulated sugar
- 1/4 cup packed light brown sugar
- 1/2 teaspoon ground cinnamon
- 1/4 teaspoon ground nutmeg
- 1/4 teaspoon salt
- Toasted coconut* and pineapple wedges (optional)

****To toast coconut, cook and stir coconut in small skillet over medium heat until light golden brown.***

1. Combine pineapple with juice, coconut milk, evaporated milk, rice, eggs, granulated sugar, brown sugar, cinnamon, nutmeg and salt in **CROCK-POT®** slow cooker; mix well. Cover; cook on HIGH 3 to 4 hours or until thickened and rice is tender.

2. Stir until blended. Serve warm or chilled. Garnish with toasted coconut and pineapple.

Makes 8 servings

Orange Soufflé

- **6 tablespoons unsalted butter, softened, divided**
- **$1\frac{1}{4}$ cups sugar, divided**
- **Grated peel of 1 orange**
- **$\frac{1}{2}$ cup milk**
- **6 tablespoons all-purpose flour**
- **8 egg yolks**
- **6 tablespoons orange-flavored liqueur**
- **1 tablespoon vanilla**
- **10 egg whites**
- **1 teaspoon salt**

1. Grease **CROCK-POT®** slow cooker with 2 tablespoons butter. Pour in ⅓ cup sugar; turn to evenly coat bottom and sides of **CROCK-POT®** slow cooker.

2. Process ⅔ cup sugar and orange peel in food processor until orange peel is evenly ground.

3. Whisk milk and flour in medium saucepan over medium heat. Cook and stir until mixture begins to thicken. Bring to a boil, whisking constantly. Cook 30 seconds, then remove from heat. Let cool slightly.

4. Beat in egg yolks, one at a time. Add remaining 4 tablespoons butter, orange liqueur and vanilla. Let stand at room temperature 20 minutes to cool.

5. Beat egg whites in clean, dry bowl until foamy. Add salt and beat until soft peaks form. Sprinkle with remaining ¼ cup sugar and beat until stiff peaks form.

6. Fold one-fourth of beaten egg whites into cooled batter. Fold in remaining egg whites, then gently transfer to **CROCK-POT®** slow cooker. Cover; cook on HIGH 1 hour or until set. Serve immediately.

Makes 10 servings

Braised Fruited Lamb

- 6 tablespoons extra virgin olive oil
- 4 pounds lamb shanks
- 2 tablespoons salt
- 2 tablespoons black pepper
- 1 cup dried apricots
- 1 cup dried figs
- 1½ cups water
- ½ cup white vinegar or white wine
- ¼ cup raspberry jam
- ½ teaspoon ground allspice
- ½ teaspoon ground cinnamon

1. Preheat broiler. Brush oil on lamb shanks and season with salt and pepper. Place shanks in broilerproof pan and broil about 5 minutes on each side or until browned. Transfer to **CROCK-POT®** slow cooker. Add apricots and figs.

2. Combine water, vinegar, jam, allspice and cinnamon in small bowl. Pour over lamb shanks. Cover; cook on LOW 8 to 9 hours or on HIGH 4 to 5 hours.

Makes 6 to 8 servings

Moroccan-Style Lamb Shoulder Chops with Couscous

- 4 lamb blade chops (about $2\frac{1}{2}$ pounds)
- Salt and black pepper
- 1 tablespoon olive oil
- 1 onion, chopped
- 1 clove garlic, minced
- 1 teaspoon grated fresh ginger
- 1/4 teaspoon ground cinnamon
- 1/2 teaspoon ground turmeric
- 1/2 teaspoon salt
- 1/4 teaspoon black pepper
- 1 bay leaf
- 1 can (about 14 ounces) diced tomatoes, undrained
- 1 cup canned chickpeas, rinsed and drained
- 1/2 cup water
- 2 tablespoons lemon juice
- Hot cooked couscous
- Lemon wedges (optional)

1. Coat **CROCK-POT®** slow cooker with nonstick cooking spray. Season lamb chops with salt and pepper. Heat oil in large skillet over medium-high heat. Add lamb chops and brown on all sides. Transfer to **CROCK-POT®** slow cooker.

2. Add onion to skillet. Cook and stir 2 to 3 minutes or until translucent. Add garlic, ginger, cinnamon, turmeric, 1/2 teaspoon salt, 1/4 teaspoon pepper and bay leaf. Cook and stir 30 seconds. Stir in tomatoes with juice, chickpeas, water and lemon juice. Simmer 2 minutes. Pour mixture over lamb. Cover; cook on HIGH $3\frac{1}{2}$ to 4 hours or until lamb is tender.

3. Remove bay leaf. Serve lamb chops over couscous with sauce and vegetables. Serve with lemon wedges, if desired.

Makes 4 servings

Tip: Adding fresh lemon juice just before serving enhances the flavor of many dishes.

Spring Vegetable Ragoût

- **1 tablespoon olive oil**
- **2 leeks, thinly sliced**
- **3 cloves garlic, minced**
- **1 cup vegetable broth**
- **1 package (10 ounces) frozen corn**
- **1/2 pound yellow squash, halved lengthwise and cut into 1/2-inch pieces (about 1 1/4 cups)**
- **1 small bag (6 ounces) frozen edamame (soybeans), shelled**
- **1 package (4 ounces) shredded carrots**
- **3 cups cherry tomatoes, halved**
- **1 teaspoon dried tarragon**
- **1 teaspoon dried basil**
- **1 teaspoon dried oregano**
- **Salt and black pepper (optional)**
- **Minced fresh parsley (optional)**

1. Heat oil in large skillet over medium heat. Add leeks and garlic; cook and stir just until fragrant.

2. Combine leeks and garlic with broth, corn, squash, edamame, carrots, tomatoes, tarragon, basil and oregano in **CROCK-POT®** slow cooker; stir well. Cover; cook on LOW 6 to 8 hours or on HIGH 3 to 4 hours, or until vegetables are tender.

3. Season with salt and pepper, if desired. Garnish with parsley.

Makes 6 servings

Spinach Artichoke Gratin

- 2 cups (16 ounces) cottage cheese
- 2 eggs, beaten
- 4½ tablespoons grated Parmesan cheese, divided
- 1 tablespoon lemon juice
- ⅛ teaspoon black pepper
- ⅛ teaspoon ground nutmeg
- 2 packages (10 ounces each) frozen chopped spinach, thawed and squeezed dry
- ⅓ cup thinly sliced green onions
- 1 package (10 ounces) frozen artichoke hearts, thawed and halved

1. Process cottage cheese, eggs, 3 tablespoons Parmesan cheese, lemon juice, pepper and nutmeg in food processor until smooth.

2. Coat **CROCK-POT®** slow cooker with nonstick cooking spray. Combine spinach, cottage cheese mixture and green onions in large bowl. Spread half of mixture in **CROCK-POT®** slow cooker.

3. Pat artichoke halves dry with paper towels. Place in single layer over spinach mixture. Sprinkle with remaining Parmesan cheese. Cover with remaining spinach mixture. Cook, covered, with lid slightly ajar to allow excess moisture to escape, on LOW 3 to 3½ hours or on HIGH 2 to 2½ hours.

Makes 6 servings

Ham and Potato Casserole

- 1½ pounds red potatoes, peeled and sliced
- 8 ounces thinly sliced ham
- 2 poblano chile peppers, cut into thin strips
- 2 tablespoons olive oil
- 1 tablespoon dried oregano
- ¼ teaspoon salt
- 1 cup (4 ounces) shredded Monterey Jack or pepper jack cheese
- 2 tablespoons finely chopped fresh cilantro

1. Combine all ingredients except cheese and cilantro in **CROCK-POT®** slow cooker; mix well. Cover; cook on LOW 7 hours or on HIGH 4 hours.

2. Transfer potato mixture to serving dish; sprinkle with cheese and cilantro. Let stand 3 minutes or until cheese is melted.

Makes 6 to 7 servings

Manchego Eggplant

- 4 **eggplants**
- 1 **cup all-purpose flour**
- 2 **tablespoons olive oil**
- 1 **jar (about 26 ounces) roasted garlic pasta sauce**
- 2 **tablespoons Italian seasoning, divided**
- 3½ **ounces grated manchego cheese, divided**
- 1 **jar (24 ounces) roasted eggplant marinara, divided**

1. Peel eggplants and slice horizontally into ¾-inch-thick pieces. Place flour in shallow bowl. Dredge each slice of eggplant in flour to coat.

2. Heat oil in large skillet over medium-high heat. Lightly brown eggplant on both sides in batches.

3. Pour thin layer of roasted garlic pasta sauce into **CROCK-POT®** slow cooker. Top with layer of eggplant slices, Italian seasoning, cheese and roasted eggplant marinara. Repeat layers until all ingredients have been used.

4. Cover; cook on HIGH 2 hours.

Makes 8 to 10 servings

Finer Fare

Sauvignon Blanc Beef with Beets and Thyme

- 1 pound red or yellow beets, quartered
- 2 tablespoons extra virgin olive oil
- 1 beef chuck roast (about 3 pounds)
- 1 yellow onion, peeled and quartered
- 2 cloves garlic, minced
- 5 sprigs fresh thyme
- 1 bay leaf
- 2 whole cloves
- 1 cup chicken broth
- 1 cup Sauvignon Blanc or other white wine
- 2 tablespoons tomato paste
- Salt and black pepper

1. Layer beets evenly in **CROCK-POT®** slow cooker.

2. Heat oil in large skillet over medium heat until hot. Sear roast 4 to 5 minutes on each side. Add onion and garlic during last few minutes of searing. Transfer to **CROCK-POT®** slow cooker.

3. Add thyme, bay leaf and cloves. Combine broth, wine, tomato paste, salt and pepper in medium bowl; mix well. Pour over roast and beets. Cover; cook on LOW 8 to 10 hours or until roast is fork-tender and beets are tender. Remove bay leaf before serving.

Makes 6 servings

Sausage and Swiss Chard Stuffed Mushrooms

2 packages (6 ounces each) baby portobello mushrooms or large brown stuffing mushrooms*
4 tablespoons extra virgin olive oil, divided
1/2 teaspoon salt, divided
1/2 teaspoon black pepper, divided
1/2 pound bulk pork sausage
1/2 onion, finely chopped
2 cups chopped Swiss chard
1/4 teaspoon dried thyme
2 tablespoons seasoned bread crumbs
1 1/2 cups chicken broth, divided
2 tablespoons grated Parmesan cheese
2 tablespoons chopped fresh parsley

****Use "baby bellas" or cremini mushrooms. Do not substitute white button mushrooms.***

1. Coat **CROCK-POT®** slow cooker with nonstick cooking spray. Wipe mushrooms clean, remove stems and hollow out mushroom caps. Brush mushrooms inside and out with 3 tablespoons oil. Season with 1/4 teaspoon salt and 1/4 teaspoon pepper; set aside.

2. Heat remaining 1 tablespoon oil in medium skillet over medium heat. Add sausage; cook and stir until browned. Transfer to medium bowl with slotted spoon.

3. Add onion to skillet. Cook 3 minutes or until translucent, stirring to scrape up browned bits. Stir in chard and thyme. Cook until chard is just wilted, about 1 to 2 minutes.

4. Remove skillet from heat. Add sausage, bread crumbs, 1 tablespoon broth, remaining 1/4 teaspoon salt and 1/4 teaspoon pepper; mix well. Scoop 1 tablespoon stuffing into each mushroom cap. Divide remaining stuffing evenly among mushrooms.

5. Pour remaining broth into **CROCK-POT®** slow cooker. Arrange stuffed mushrooms on bottom. Cover; cook on HIGH 3 hours or until mushrooms are tender. Remove mushrooms with slotted spoon; discard cooking liquid. Combine cheese and parsley in small bowl and sprinkle onto mushrooms.

Makes 6 to 8 servings

Variation: If desired, place a small square of sliced Swiss cheese on each mushroom and cook 15 minutes or until cheese is melted. Proceed as directed.

Chicken Liver Pâté

Pâté

1½ pounds chicken livers, trimmed
1 onion, thinly sliced
3 sprigs fresh thyme
2 cloves garlic, crushed
¼ teaspoon salt
1 tablespoon water
3 tablespoons cold butter, cut into 4 pieces
2 tablespoons whipping cream
2 tablespoons sherry

Garnish

½ shallot, minced (optional)
2 tablespoons chopped fresh parsley (optional)
1 tablespoon sherry vinegar (optional)
⅛ teaspoon sugar
Salt and black pepper

Melba toast or toast points

1. Rinse chicken livers and pat dry. Place in **CROCK-POT®** slow cooker. Add onion, thyme, garlic, salt and water. Cover; cook on LOW 2 hours.

2. Remove thyme sprigs and discard. Pour remaining ingredients from **CROCK-POT®** slow cooker into strainer and cool until just warm to the touch. Transfer to food processor and pulse just long enough to coarsely chop livers. Add butter, one piece at a time, pulsing just enough each time to combine.

3. Add cream and sherry and pulse to combine. Transfer to serving bowl and serve immediately. Alternatively, transfer to a small loaf pan, pressing plastic wrap to surface of pâté. Refrigerate overnight, tightly wrapped in additional plastic wrap. Unmold pâté and slice to serve.

4. Stir together shallot, if desired, parsley, vinegar, sugar, salt and pepper in small bowl. Set aside 5 minutes, then spoon over pâté. Serve with Melba toast.

Makes about 2½ cups

Finer Fare

Steamed Artichokes with Three Sauces

4 artichokes, trimmed and cut in half

½ lemon, juiced

Dipping Sauces (recipes follow)

Place trimmed artichokes cut side down in bottom of **CROCK-POT®** slow cooker. Add enough water to come halfway up artichokes; add lemon juice. Cover; cook on LOW 6 hours. Serve with one or more Dipping Sauces.

Makes 8 servings

Tarragon Browned Butter Dipping Sauce

1 cup (2 sticks) butter

4 teaspoons dried tarragon *or* ¼ cup finely chopped fresh tarragon

Melt butter in medium saucepan over medium heat. Cook, swirling butter in saucepan over heat until butter is light brown. Remove from heat and stir in tarragon.

Cream Cheese-Bacon Dipping Sauce

4 ounces cream cheese

1 cup whipping cream

½ teaspoon black pepper

8 slices bacon, cooked and finely chopped

Whisk cream cheese and cream in medium saucepan over medium heat until smooth. Stir in pepper and bacon.

Garlic-Herb Butter Dipping Sauce

1 cup (2 sticks) butter

8 cloves garlic, crushed

½ cup chopped fresh herbs such as parsley, tarragon or chives

Melt butter in medium saucepan over medium heat. Add garlic and cook, stirring frequently, until garlic is golden brown. Remove from heat. Strain garlic from sauce and stir in herbs.

Steamed Artichokes with Three Sauces

Spinach, Crab and Artichoke Dip

- 1 can ($6\frac{1}{2}$ ounces) crabmeat, drained and shredded
- 1 package (10 ounces) frozen chopped spinach, thawed and squeezed nearly dry
- 1 package (8 ounces) cream cheese
- 1 jar (about 6 ounces) marinated artichoke hearts, drained and finely chopped
- 1/4 teaspoon hot pepper sauce
- Melba toast or whole grain crackers (optional)

Pick out and discard any shell or cartilage from crabmeat. Combine crabmeat, spinach, cream cheese, artichokes and hot pepper sauce in $1\frac{1}{2}$-quart **CROCK-POT®** slow cooker. Cover; cook on HIGH $1\frac{1}{2}$ to 2 hours or until heated through, stirring after 1 hour. Serve with Melba toast, if desired.

Makes about $2\frac{1}{2}$ cups

Tomato Topping for Bruschetta

- **6 tomatoes, peeled, seeded and diced**
- **2 stalks celery, trimmed and chopped**
- **2 shallots, chopped**
- **4 peperoncini peppers, chopped***
- **2 teaspoons tomato paste**
- **1 teaspoon salt**
- **1/2 teaspoon black pepper**
- **2 tablespoons olive oil**
- **8 slices country bread or other large round bread**
- **2 cloves garlic**

Peperoncini are pickled peppers sold in jars with brine. They're available in the supermarket condiment aisle.

1. Drain any tomato juices. Combine tomatoes, celery, shallots, peperoncini, tomato paste, salt, black pepper and oil in **CROCK-POT®** slow cooker. Cover; cook on LOW 45 minutes to 1 hour.

2. Toast bread. Immediately rub with garlic. Spread tomato topping on bread. Serve immediately.

Makes about 2 cups

Variation: To serve as a main dish, omit bread and garlic, and toss tomato topping with cooked penne pasta. You may also spoon the topping over roasted chicken breasts as a flavorful sauce.

Shrimp and Pepper Bisque

- 1 bag (12 ounces) frozen bell pepper blend, thawed
- 1/2 pound frozen cauliflower florets, thawed
- 1 stalk celery, sliced
- 1 tablespoon seafood seasoning
- 1/2 teaspoon dried thyme
- 1 can (about 14 ounces) chicken broth
- 12 ounces medium raw shrimp, peeled and deveined
- 2 cups half-and-half
- 2 to 3 green onions, finely chopped

1. Combine bell pepper blend, cauliflower, celery, seafood seasoning, thyme and broth in **CROCK-POT®** slow cooker. Cover; cook on LOW 8 hours or on HIGH 4 hours.

2. Stir in shrimp. Cover; cook 15 minutes or until shrimp are pink and opaque. Process soup in batches in blender or food processor until smooth. Return to **CROCK-POT®** slow cooker. Stir in half-and-half. Ladle into bowls and sprinkle with green onions.

Makes 4 servings

Tip: For a creamier, smoother consistency, strain through several layers of damp cheesecloth.

Warm Blue Crab Bruschetta

- 4 cups diced, seeded, peeled plum tomatoes
- 1 cup diced white onion
- 1/3 cup olive oil
- 2 tablespoons sugar
- 2 tablespoons balsamic vinegar
- 2 teaspoons minced garlic
- 1/2 teaspoon dried oregano
- 1 pound lump blue crabmeat
- 1 1/2 teaspoons kosher salt
- 1/2 teaspoon cracked black pepper
- 1/3 cup minced fresh basil
- 2 baguettes, sliced and toasted

1. Combine tomatoes, onion, oil, sugar, vinegar, garlic and oregano in **CROCK-POT®** slow cooker. Cover; cook on LOW 2 hours.

2. Pick out and discard any shell or cartilage from crabmeat. Add crabmeat, salt and pepper to **CROCK-POT®** slow cooker. Stir gently to mix, taking care not to break up crabmeat. Cook on LOW 1 hour.

3. Fold in basil. Serve on toasted baguette slices.

Makes 16 servings

Serving Suggestion: Crab topping can also be served on Melba toast or whole grain crackers.

Stuffed Baby Bell Peppers

- 1 tablespoon extra virgin olive oil
- 1/2 onion, chopped
- 1/2 pound ground beef, chicken or turkey
- 1/2 cup cooked white rice
- 3 tablespoons chopped fresh parsley
- 2 tablespoons lemon juice
- 1 tablespoon dried dill weed
- 1 tablespoon tomato paste, divided
- 1/2 teaspoon salt
- 1/8 teaspoon black pepper
- 24 yellow and red baby bell peppers
- 1/4 cup vegetable, chicken or beef broth

1. Heat oil in medium skillet over medium heat. Add onion and cook until translucent, stirring occasionally.

2. Add ground beef and cook 6 to 8 minutes or until browned, stirring to break up meat. Drain fat. Transfer meat to large bowl. Add rice, parsley, lemon juice, dill, 1½ teaspoons tomato paste, salt and black pepper. Mix until well combined. Set aside.

3. Cut small slit in side of each baby bell pepper and run under cold water to wash out seeds. Fill each bell pepper with 2 to 3 teaspoons seasoned beef. Place bell peppers in **CROCK-POT®** slow cooker, slit side up. Add broth and remaining tomato paste. Cover; cook on LOW 5 hours or on HIGH 2½ hours.

Makes 16 to 18 servings

Chicken Tagine with Lemon and Olives

1 onion, finely chopped
4 cloves garlic, minced
Peel and juice of 1 lemon
2 teaspoons crushed dried rosemary *or* 2 tablespoons chopped fresh rosemary
1 teaspoon dried thyme *or* 1 tablespoon fresh thyme
2 tablespoons butter, cut into small pieces
4 chicken leg quarters
20 pitted green olives, crushed
2 tablespoons all-purpose flour
2 tablespoons water

1. Combine onions, garlic, lemon peel and juice, rosemary and thyme in **CROCK-POT®** slow cooker. Top with butter, chicken and olives. Cover; cook on LOW 5 to 6 hours.

2. Remove chicken. Turn **CROCK-POT®** slow cooker to HIGH. Combine flour and water in small bowl. Whisk into **CROCK-POT®** slow cooker until sauce is thickened slightly.

Makes 4 servings

Saffron-Scented Shrimp Paella

- 3 tablespoons olive oil, divided
- $1\frac{1}{2}$ cups chopped onions
- 4 cloves garlic, thinly sliced
- Salt
- 1 cup roasted red bell pepper, diced
- 1 cup chopped tomato
- 1 bay leaf
- Pinch saffron
- 1 cup white wine
- 8 cups chicken broth
- 4 cups rice
- 25 large shrimp, peeled and deveined
- White pepper

1. Heat 2 tablespoons oil in large skillet over medium heat. Add onions, garlic and salt; cook and stir 5 minutes until onions are translucent. Add bell pepper, tomato, bay leaf and saffron; cook and stir until heated through. Add wine; cook until liquid is reduced by half. Add broth. Bring to a simmer. Stir in rice. Transfer to **CROCK-POT®** slow cooker. Cover; cook on HIGH 30 minutes to 1 hour or until all liquid is absorbed.

2. Toss shrimp in remaining 1 tablespoon oil; season with salt and white pepper. Place shrimp on rice in **CROCK-POT®** slow cooker. Cover; cook about 10 minutes or until shrimp are opaque. Remove bay leaf before serving.

Makes 4 to 6 servings

Simmered Napa Cabbage with Dried Apricots

- **4 cups Napa cabbage or green cabbage, cored, cleaned and sliced thin**
- **1 cup chopped dried apricots**
- **1/4 cup clover honey**
- **2 tablespoons orange juice**
- **1/2 cup dry red wine**
- **Salt and black pepper**
- **Grated orange peel (optional)**

1. Combine cabbage and apricots in **CROCK-POT®** slow cooker. Toss to mix well.

2. Combine honey and orange juice in small bowl until smooth. Drizzle over cabbage. Add wine. Cover; cook on LOW 5 to 6 hours or on HIGH 2 to 3 hours, or until cabbage is tender.

3. Season with salt and pepper. Garnish with orange peel.

Makes 4 servings

Spicy Thai Coconut Soup

- 2 cups chicken broth
- 1 can (about 14 ounces) light coconut milk
- 1 tablespoon minced fresh ginger
- 1/2 to 1 teaspoon red curry paste
- 3 cups coarsely shredded cooked chicken (about 12 ounces)
- 1 can (15 ounces) straw mushrooms, drained
- 1 can (about 8 ounces) baby corn, drained
- 2 tablespoons lime juice
- 1/4 cup chopped fresh cilantro

1. Combine broth, coconut milk, ginger and red curry paste in **CROCK-POT®** slow cooker. Add chicken, mushrooms and corn.

2. Cover; cook on HIGH 2 to 3 hours. Stir in lime juice and sprinkle with cilantro just before serving.

Makes 4 servings

Note: Red curry paste can be found in jars in the Asian food section of large grocery stores. Spice levels can vary among brands. Start with 1/2 teaspoon, then add more as desired.

Ham and Sage Stuffed Cornish Hens

- **1 cup plus 3 tablespoons sliced celery, divided**
- **1 cup sliced leek (white part only)**
- **2 tablespoons butter, divided**
- **1/4 cup finely diced onion**
- **1/4 cup diced smoked ham or prosciutto**
- **1 cup seasoned stuffing mix**
- **1 cup chicken broth**
- **1 tablespoon finely chopped fresh sage leaves *or* 1 teaspoon ground sage**
- **4 Cornish hens (about 1 1/2 pounds each)**
- **Salt**
- **Black pepper**

1. Coat **CROCK-POT®** slow cooker with nonstick cooking spray. Combine 1 cup celery and leek in **CROCK-POT®** slow cooker.

2. Melt 1 tablespoon butter in large nonstick skillet over medium heat. Add remaining 3 tablespoons celery, onion and ham. Cook 5 minutes or until onion is soft, stirring frequently. Stir in stuffing mix, broth and sage. Transfer mixture to medium bowl.

3. Rinse hens and pat dry; sprinkle inside and out with salt and pepper. Gently spoon stuffing into hens. Tie hens' drumsticks together with kitchen twine.

4. Melt remaining 1 tablespoon butter in same skillet over medium-high heat. Place 2 hens, breast sides down, in skillet and cook until brown. Transfer to prepared **CROCK-POT®** slow cooker. Repeat with remaining hens. Cover; cook on LOW 5 to 6 hours or on HIGH 3 to 4 hours. Remove twine and place hens on serving platter with vegetables; spoon cooking liquid over hens.

Makes 4 servings

Braised Sea Bass with Aromatic Vegetables

- **2 tablespoons butter or olive oil**
- **2 bulbs fennel, thinly sliced**
- **3 carrots, julienned**
- **3 leeks, cleaned and thinly sliced**
- **Kosher salt and black pepper**
- **6 sea bass fillets or other firm white fish (2 to 3 pounds total)**

1. Melt butter in large skillet over medium-high heat. Add fennel, carrots and leeks. Cook and stir until beginning to soften and lightly brown. Season with salt and pepper.

2. Arrange half of vegetables in bottom of **CROCK-POT®** slow cooker.

3. Season fish with salt and pepper and place on vegetables in **CROCK-POT®** slow cooker. Top with remaining vegetables.

4. Cover and cook on LOW 2 to 3 hours or on HIGH 1 to 1½ hours or until fish is opaque.

Makes 6 servings

Wild Rice and Dried Cherry Risotto

- 1 cup dry-roasted salted peanuts
- 2 tablespoons sesame oil, divided
- 1 cup chopped onion
- 6 ounces uncooked wild rice
- 1 cup diced carrots
- 1 cup chopped green or red bell pepper
- 1/2 cup dried cherries
- 1/8 to 1/4 teaspoon red pepper flakes
- 4 cups hot water
- 1/4 cup teriyaki or soy sauce
- 1 teaspoon salt

1. Coat **CROCK-POT®** slow cooker with nonstick cooking spray. Heat large skillet over medium-high heat. Add peanuts. Cook and stir 2 to 3 minutes or until peanuts begin to brown. Transfer peanuts to plate; set aside.

2. Heat 2 teaspoons oil in skillet. Add onion. Cook and stir 6 minutes or until richly browned. Transfer to **CROCK-POT®** slow cooker. Stir in wild rice, carrots, bell pepper, cherries, red pepper flakes and water. Cover; cook on HIGH 3 hours.

3. Uncover; let stand 15 minutes or until all liquid is absorbed. Stir in peanuts, remaining oil, teriyaki sauce and salt.

Makes 8 to 10 servings

Slow-Roasted Potatoes

- **16 new red potatoes**
- **3 tablespoons butter, cut into small pieces**
- **1 teaspoon paprika**
- **½ teaspoon salt**
- **¼ teaspoon garlic powder**
- **Black pepper**

Combine all ingredients in **CROCK-POT®** slow cooker; mix well. Cover; cook on LOW 7 hours or on HIGH 4 hours. Remove potatoes with slotted spoon to serving dish; cover with foil to keep warm. Add 1 to 2 tablespoons water to cooking liquid and stir until well blended. Pour over potatoes.

Makes 3 to 4 servings

Pork Roast with Dijon Tarragon Glaze

- 2 tablespoons Dijon mustard
- 1 teaspoon minced fresh tarragon
- 2 tablespoons lemon juice
- 1/3 cup chicken or vegetable broth
- 1½ to 2 pounds boneless pork loin, visible fat removed
- 1 teaspoon ground paprika
- ½ teaspoon black pepper

1. Combine mustard, tarragon, lemon juice and broth in small bowl; set aside. Sprinkle roast with paprika and pepper. Place roast in **CROCK-POT®** slow cooker. Spoon glaze evenly over roast. Cover; cook on LOW 6 to 8 hours or on HIGH 3 to 4 hours.

2. Remove roast from **CROCK-POT®** slow cooker; let stand 15 minutes before slicing.

Makes 4 to 6 servings

Fennel Braised with Tomato

- 2 bulbs fennel
- 1 tablespoon extra virgin olive oil
- 1 onion, sliced
- 1 clove garlic, sliced
- 4 tomatoes, chopped
- 2/3 cup vegetable broth or water
- 3 tablespoons dry white wine or vegetable broth
- 1 tablespoon chopped fresh marjoram *or* 1 teaspoon dried marjoram
- 1/4 teaspoon salt
- 1/4 teaspoon black pepper

1. Trim stems and bottoms from fennel bulbs, reserving green leafy tops for garnish. Cut each bulb lengthwise into 4 wedges.

2. Heat oil in large skillet over medium heat. Add fennel, onion and garlic; cook and stir 5 minutes or until onion is soft and translucent.

3. Combine all ingredients in **CROCK-POT®** slow cooker. Cover; cook on LOW 2 to 3 hours or on HIGH 1 to 1½ hours or until vegetables are tender, stirring occasionally. Garnish with fennel leaves.

Makes 6 servings

Pears with Apricot-Ginger Sauce

- **1/4 cup water**
- **4 whole firm pears (about 2 pounds total), peeled with stems attached**
- **1 tablespoon lemon juice**
- **2 tablespoons apricot fruit spread**
- **1 teaspoon grated fresh ginger**
- **1/2 teaspoon cornstarch**
- **1/2 teaspoon vanilla**

1. Coat **CROCK-POT®** slow cooker with nonstick cooking spray. Add water. Arrange pears stem side up. Spoon lemon juice over pears. Cover; cook on HIGH 2½ hours.

2. Remove pears; set aside.

3. Combine fruit spread, ginger, cornstarch and vanilla in small bowl; stir until cornstarch dissolves. Add mixture to water in **CROCK-POT®** slow cooker, whisking until blended. Cover; cook on HIGH 15 minutes or until sauce thickens slightly. Spoon sauce over pears. Serve warm or at room temperature.

Makes 4 servings

Brioche and Amber Rum Custard

- 2 tablespoons unsalted butter
- 3½ cups whipping cream
- 4 eggs
- ½ cup packed dark brown sugar
- ⅓ cup amber or light rum
- 2 teaspoons vanilla
- 1 loaf (20 to 22 ounces) brioche, torn into pieces*
- ½ cup coarsely chopped pecans
- Caramel or butterscotch topping (optional)

**If desired, trim and discard heels.*

1. Generously grease **CROCK-POT®** slow cooker with butter. Combine cream, eggs, brown sugar, rum and vanilla in large bowl; stir well.

2. Place one-fourth of brioche pieces in bottom of prepared **CROCK-POT®** slow cooker. Ladle one fourth of cream mixture over brioche. Sprinkle with one third of pecans. Repeat twice.

3. Cover; cook on LOW 3 to 3½ hours or on HIGH 1¾ to 2 hours or until custard is set and tester inserted into center comes out clean.

4. Serve warm. Drizzle with caramel or butterscotch topping, if desired.

Makes 4 to 6 servings

Bittersweet Chocolate-Espresso Crème Brûlée

- **1/2 cup chopped bittersweet chocolate**
- **5 egg yolks**
- **1 3/4 cups heavy cream**
- **1/4 cup espresso**
- **1/2 cup granulated sugar**
- **1/4 cup Demerara or raw sugar**

1. Arrange five 6-ounce ramekins or custard cups inside **CROCK-POT®** slow cooker. Pour enough water to come halfway up sides of ramekins (taking care to keep water out of ramekins). Divide chocolate among ramekins.

2. Whisk egg yolks briefly in medium bowl; set aside. Heat cream, espresso and granulated sugar in small saucepan over medium heat, stirring constantly, until mixture begins to boil. Pour hot cream in thin, steady stream into egg yolks, whisking constantly. Pour through fine mesh strainer into clean bowl.

3. Ladle into prepared ramekins. Cover; cook on HIGH 1 to 2 hours or until custard is set around edges but still soft in centers. Carefully remove and cool to room temperature, then cover and refrigerate until serving.

4. Sprinkle tops of custards with Demerara sugar just before serving; melt with kitchen torch. Serve immediately.

Makes 5 servings

Fun Finger Foods

Sweet Hot Chicken Wings

1 1/2 pounds chicken wings
6 tablespoons salsa, plus additional for serving
1/3 cup honey
2 1/2 tablespoons soy sauce
2 tablespoons Dijon mustard
1 tablespoon vegetable oil
1 1/2 teaspoons grated fresh ginger
1/4 teaspoon grated orange peel
1/4 teaspoon grated lemon peel
Ranch dressing (optional)

1. Cut off and discard wing tips from chicken. Cut each wing in half at joint. Place wings in 13×9-inch baking dish.

2. Combine salsa, honey, soy sauce, mustard, oil, ginger, orange peel and lemon peel in small bowl; mix well. Pour over chicken wings. Cover; marinate in refrigerator at least 6 hours or overnight.

3. Preheat oven to 400°F. Place chicken wings in single layer on foil-lined, 15×10-inch jelly-roll pan. Pour marinade evenly over chicken wings. Bake 40 to 45 minutes until brown. Transfer as many wings to serving platter or **CROCK-POT® LITTLE DIPPER®** slow cooker as will fit. Reserve and keep warm any extra wings, refilling **CROCK-POT® LITTLE DIPPER®** slow cooker as space allows. Serve with additional salsa or ranch dressing for dipping.

Makes about 3 dozen servings

Mini Carnitas Tacos

- 1½ pounds boneless pork loin, cut into 1-inch cubes
- 1 onion, finely chopped
- ½ cup chicken broth
- 1 tablespoon chili powder
- 2 teaspoons ground cumin
- 1 teaspoon dried oregano
- ½ teaspoon minced chipotle pepper in adobo sauce
- ½ cup pico de gallo
- 2 tablespoons chopped fresh cilantro
- ½ teaspoon salt
- 12 (6-inch) flour or corn tortillas
- ¾ cup shredded sharp Cheddar cheese (optional)
- 3 tablespoons sour cream (optional)

1. Combine pork, onion, broth, chili powder, cumin, oregano and chipotle pepper in **CROCK-POT®** slow cooker. Cover; cook on LOW 6 hours or on HIGH 3 hours, or until pork is very tender. Pour off excess cooking liquid.

2. Shred pork with two forks; stir in pico de gallo, cilantro and salt. Cover and keep warm on LOW or WARM until serving.

3. Cut 3 circles from each tortilla with 2-inch biscuit cutter. Top each with pork and garnish with cheese and sour cream. Serve warm.

Makes 36 mini tacos

Tip: Carnitas, or "little meats" in Spanish, are a festive way to spice up any gathering. Carnitas traditionally include a large amount of lard, but slow cooking makes the dish more healthful by eliminating the need to add lard, oil or fat, while keeping the meat tender and tasteful.

Soy-Braised Chicken Wings

- 1/4 cup dry sherry
- 1/4 cup soy sauce
- 3 tablespoons sugar
- 2 tablespoons cornstarch
- 2 tablespoons minced garlic, divided
- 2 teaspoons red pepper flakes
- 12 chicken wings (about 2 1/2 pounds), tips removed and cut in half at the joint
- 2 tablespoons vegetable oil, divided
- 3 green onions, cut into 1-inch pieces
- 1/4 cup chicken broth
- 1 teaspoon sesame oil
- 1 tablespoon sesame seeds, toasted*

***To toast sesame seeds, place in small skillet. Shake skillet over medium-low heat about 3 minutes or until seeds begin to pop and turn golden. Remove from heat.**

1. Combine sherry, soy sauce, sugar, cornstarch, 1 tablespoon garlic and red pepper flakes in large bowl; mix well. Reserve 1/4 cup marinade in separate bowl. Stir chicken wings into remaining marinade. Cover and marinate in refrigerator overnight, turning once or twice.

2. Drain wings; discard marinade. Heat 1 tablespoon oil in wok or large skillet over high heat 1 minute. Add half of wings; cook 3 to 4 minutes or until wings are brown on all sides, turning occasionally. Remove with slotted spoon to **CROCK-POT®** slow cooker. Repeat with remaining vegetable oil and wings.

3. Add remaining 1 tablespoon garlic and green onions to wok; cook and stir 30 seconds. Stir in broth and pour over wings. Cover; cook on HIGH 2 hours or until wings are cooked through.

4. Transfer as many wings to serving platter or **CROCK-POT® LITTLE DIPPER®** slow cooker with slotted spoon as will fit. Reserve and keep warm any extra wings, refilling **CROCK-POT® LITTLE DIPPER®** slow cooker as space allows. Add sesame oil to reserved marinade; mix well. Pour over wings; sprinkle with sesame seeds. Serve immediately.

Makes 2 dozen wings

Feta and Mint Spread

- 1/2 cup plain Greek yogurt
- 3 ounces feta cheese, crumbled
- 2 ounces cream cheese, cubed
- 2 tablespoons extra virgin olive oil
- 1 small garlic clove, crushed to a paste
- 1 tablespoon chopped fresh mint
- 1/2 teaspoon grated fresh lemon peel
- Toasted Pita Chips (recipe below)
- Carrot and celery sticks

Grease **CROCK-POT® LITTLE DIPPER®** slow cooker. Add yogurt, feta cheese, cream cheese, oil and garlic; mix well. Cover; heat 1 hour until cheese is melted. Stir in mint and lemon peel. Serve with Toasted Pita Chips, carrot sticks and celery sticks.

Makes about 2 cups

Toasted Pita Chips

- 3 (6-inch) pita bread rounds
- 1 tablespoon extra virgin olive oil
- 1/2 teaspoon dried oregano
- 1/4 teaspoon ground cumin
- 1/8 teaspoon salt

1. Preheat oven to 375°F.
2. Brush one side of each pita round with oil. Sprinkle with oregano, cumin and salt. Cut each pita into 12 wedges. Place on baking sheet seasoned side up. Bake 8 minutes or until lightly browned. Cool.

Makes 36 chips

Chipotle Chili con Queso Dip

- 10 ounces pasteurized process cheese product, cubed
- 1/4 cup mild chunky salsa
- 1/2 chipotle pepper in adobo sauce, finely chopped*
- 1/2 teaspoon Worcestershire sauce
- 1/8 teaspoon chili powder
- Pretzels
- Tortilla chips

**Use more to taste.*

1. Grease **CROCK-POT® LITTLE DIPPER®** slow cooker. Combine cheese, salsa, chipotle pepper, Worcestershire sauce and chili powder in **CROCK-POT® LITTLE DIPPER®** slow cooker. Cover; heat 1 hour.

2. Stir well. Replace cover; heat 30 minutes or until cheese is melted. Stir until smooth. Serve with pretzels and tortilla chips.

Makes about 1 1/2 cups

Pancetta Horseradish Dip

- **3 slices pancetta**
- **8 ounces cream cheese, cubed**
- **¾ cup shredded Swiss cheese**
- **¼ cup whipping cream**
- **¼ cup chopped green onions**
- **1 tablespoon prepared horseradish, drained**
- **1 teaspoon Worcestershire sauce**
- **½ teaspoon Dijon mustard**
- **Additional green onions (optional)**
- **Potato chips**
- **Vegetable chips**
- **Seeded flat breads**

1. Heat small skillet over medium heat. Add pancetta and cook 4 minutes or until crisp, turning occasionally. Drain on paper towels. Let cool then crumble and set aside.

2. Grease **CROCK-POT® LITTLE DIPPER®** slow cooker. Add cream cheese, Swiss cheese, cream, ¼ cup green onions, horseradish, Worcestershire sauce and mustard. Cover; heat 1 hour then stir. Cover; heat 30 minutes longer or until cheese is melted.

3. Stir in all but 2 teaspoons pancetta. Sprinkle remaining pancetta and additional green onions on top. Serve with potato chips, vegetable chips and seeded flat breads.

Makes about 1½ cups

Creamy Cheesy Spinach Dip

- 1 tablespoon olive oil
- 1/2 cup diced onion
- 1 package (10 ounces) frozen chopped spinach, thawed, undrained
- 6 ounces pasteurized process cheese spread with jalapeño peppers, cubed
- 3 tablespoons milk
- 1/2 teaspoon hot pepper sauce
- 1/2 teaspoon garlic powder
- 1/8 teaspoon salt
- 1/8 teaspoon black pepper
- Crackers and cherry tomatoes

1. Heat oil in medium saucepan over medium-high heat. Add onion; cook 5 minutes or until translucent, stirring occasionally. Stir in remaining ingredients except crackers and cherry tomatoes. Bring to a boil over medium-high heat. Reduce heat and simmer, uncovered, 5 minutes or until onion is tender.

2. Coat **CROCK-POT® LITTLE DIPPER®** slow cooker with nonstick cooking spray. Fill with warm dip. Serve with crackers and cherry tomatoes.

Makes 1 3/4 cups

Caramelized Onion Dip

- **1 tablespoon olive oil**
- **1½ cups chopped sweet onion**
- **1 teaspoon sugar**
- **⅛ teaspoon dried thyme**
- **¼ teaspoon salt**
- **2 ounces cream cheese, cubed**
- **½ cup sour cream**
- **⅓ cup mayonnaise**
- **⅓ cup shredded Swiss cheese**
- **¼ teaspoon beef soup base or beef bouillon granules**
- **Potato chips**
- **Carrot sticks**
- **Pretzels**

1. Heat oil in medium skillet over medium heat. Add onion, sugar and thyme; cook 12 minutes or until golden, stirring occasionally. Stir in salt.

2. Grease **CROCK-POT® LITTLE DIPPER®** slow cooker. Add onion mixture, cream cheese, sour cream, mayonnaise, Swiss cheese and beef base; mix well. Cover; heat 1 hour or until warm; mix well. Serve with potato chips, carrot sticks and pretzels.

Makes 12 servings

Chesapeake Bay Crab Dip

- 1 can ($6^{1}/_{2}$ ounces) crabmeat, well drained
- 3 ounces cream cheese, cubed
- $^{1}/_{3}$ cup sour cream
- 3 tablespoons mayonnaise
- 2 tablespoons finely chopped onion
- $^{1}/_{2}$ teaspoon Chesapeake Bay seasoning
- $^{1}/_{4}$ teaspoon hot pepper sauce
- 1 tablespoon chopped fresh chives
- Multi-grain crackers
- Toasted baguette slices

1. Grease **CROCK-POT® LITTLE DIPPER®** slow cooker. Pick out and discard any shell or cartilage from crabmeat. Add crabmeat, cream cheese, sour cream, mayonnaise, onion, Chesapeake Bay seasoning and hot pepper sauce; stir. Cover; heat 1 hour.

2. Stir well. Cover; heat 30 minutes. Stir in chives. Serve with multi-grain crackers and toasted baguette slices.

Makes about $1^{1}/_{2}$ cups

Curried Snack Mix

- 3 tablespoons butter
- 2 tablespoons packed light brown sugar
- 1½ teaspoons hot curry powder
- ¼ teaspoon salt
- ¼ teaspoon ground cumin
- 2 cups rice cereal squares
- 1 cup walnut halves
- 1 cup dried cranberries

Melt butter in large skillet. Add brown sugar, curry powder, salt and cumin; mix well. Add cereal, walnuts and cranberries; stir to coat. Transfer mixture to **CROCK-POT®** slow cooker. Cover; cook on LOW 3 hours. Uncover; cook 30 minutes.

Makes 16 servings

Spicy Cheddar Dip

- 2 slices bacon, chopped
- 4 ounces cream cheese, cubed
- 1 cup shredded extra sharp Cheddar cheese
- 1/2 jalapeño pepper, finely chopped*
- 1/2 teaspoon hot pepper sauce
- 3 tablespoons sour cream
- Tortilla chips
- Pretzel sticks

****Jalapeño peppers can sting and irritate the skin, so wear rubber gloves when handling peppers and do not touch your eyes.***

1. Heat small skillet over medium heat. Add bacon and cook 4 minutes or until crisp, stirring occasionally. Transfer with slotted spoon to paper towel-lined plate.

2. Grease **CROCK-POT® LITTLE DIPPER®** slow cooker. Combine cream cheese, Cheddar cheese, jalapeño, hot pepper sauce and bacon in **CROCK-POT® LITTLE DIPPER®** slow cooker. Cover; heat 1 hour. Stir in sour cream. Cover; heat 30 minutes or until hot and cheese is melted. Serve with tortilla chips and pretzel sticks.

Makes about 1 1/2 cups

S'Mores Fondue

- **4 ounces semisweet chocolate chips**
- **1/2 jar (about 3 ounces) marshmallow creme**
- **3 tablespoons half-and-half**
- **1/2 teaspoon vanilla**
- **1/2 cup mini marshmallows**
- **Bananas, strawberries, chocolate-covered pretzels, graham crackers and sliced apples**

1. Combine chocolate chips, marshmallow creme and half-and-half in medium saucepan over medium heat. Cook 2 minutes or until melted and smooth, stirring constantly. Remove from heat. Stir in vanilla.

2. Coat **CROCK-POT® LITTLE DIPPER®** slow cooker with nonstick cooking spray. Fill with warm fondue. Sprinkle with mashmallows and serve with fruit, pretzels and graham crackers.

Makes 1 1/2 cups

Warm Peanut-Caramel Dip

- $^{3}/_{4}$ cup peanut butter
- $^{3}/_{4}$ cup caramel ice cream topping
- $^{1}/_{3}$ cup milk
- 1 apple, thinly sliced
- 4 large pretzel rods, cut in half

1. Combine peanut butter, caramel topping and milk in medium saucepan. Cook over medium heat until smooth and creamy, stirring occasionally.

2. Coat **CROCK-POT® LITTLE DIPPER®** slow cooker with nonstick cooking spray. Fill with warm dip. Serve with apples and pretzels.

Makes $1^{3}/_{4}$ cups

Chocolate Orange Fondue

- **½ cup whipping cream**
- **1½ tablespoons butter**
- **6 ounces 60 to 70% bittersweet chocolate, coarsely chopped**
- **⅓ cup orange liqueur**
- **¾ teaspoon vanilla**
- **Marshmallows, strawberries and pound cake cubes**

1. Bring cream and butter to a boil in medium saucepan over medium heat. Remove from heat and stir in chocolate, liqueur and vanilla until chocolate is melted. Place over medium-low heat and cook 2 minutes until smooth, stirring constantly.

2. Coat **CROCK-POT® LITTLE DIPPER®** slow cooker with nonstick cooking spray. Fill with warm fondue. Serve with marshmallows, strawberries and pound cake cubes.

Makes 1½ cups

Bagna Cauda

- 3/4 cup olive oil
- 6 tablespoons butter, softened
- 12 anchovy fillets, drained
- 6 cloves garlic, peeled
- 1/8 teaspoon red pepper flakes

Assorted dippers: endive spears, cauliflower florets, cucumber spears, carrot sticks, zucchini spears, red bell pepper pieces, sugar snap peas or crusty Italian or French bread slices

1. Place oil, butter, anchovies, garlic and red pepper flakes in food processor; process 30 seconds or until very smooth. Pour into medium saucepan over medium heat. Bring to a boil, then reduce heat to medium-low. Simmer 5 minutes.

2. Coat **CROCK-POT® LITTLE DIPPER®** slow cooker with nonstick cooking spray. Fill with warm dip. Serve with assorted dippers.

Makes 1 1/3 cups

Maple-Glazed Meatballs

- **$1\frac{1}{2}$ cups ketchup**
- **1 cup maple syrup**
- **$\frac{1}{3}$ cup soy sauce**
- **1 tablespoon quick-cooking tapioca**
- **$1\frac{1}{2}$ teaspoons ground allspice**
- **1 teaspoon dry mustard**
- **2 packages (about 16 ounces each) frozen fully cooked meatballs, partially thawed and separated**
- **1 can (20 ounces) pineapple chunks in juice, drained**

1. Combine ketchup, maple syrup, soy sauce, tapioca, allspice and mustard in **CROCK-POT®** slow cooker.

2. Carefully stir meatballs and pineapple chunks into ketchup mixture.

3. Cover; cook on LOW 5 to 6 hours. Stir before serving. Serve warm; insert cocktail picks, if desired.

Makes about 4 dozen meatballs

Tip: For a quick main dish, serve meatballs over hot cooked rice.

Warm Salsa and Goat Cheese Dip

- **1¼ cups salsa**
- **2 ounces goat cheese crumbles**
- **2 tablespoons coarsely chopped fresh cilantro**
- **Tortilla chips**

1. Bring salsa to a boil in medium saucepan over medium-high heat. Remove from heat and cool slightly.

2. Coat **CROCK-POT® LITTLE DIPPER®** slow cooker with nonstick cooking spray. Fill with heated salsa. Sprinkle with goat cheese and cilantro. (Do not stir.) Serve with tortilla chips.

Makes 1¾ cups

Variation: This dip is also great with pita chips or crisp toasted garlic bread.

Creamy Duxelles Dip

- 1 package (10 ounces) cremini or "baby bella" mushrooms
- 1 tablespoon unsalted butter
- 2 tablespoons chopped shallots
- 2 cloves garlic, minced
- 1½ teaspoons chopped fresh marjoram
- 1½ tablespoons dry sherry
- ⅛ teaspoon salt
- pinch black pepper
- 2½ tablespoons crème fraîche
- ½ tablespoon grated Parmesan cheese
- Toasted baguette slices, flat bread or multi-grain crackers

1. Place mushrooms in food processor and pulse until finely chopped.

2. Melt butter in large nonstick skillet over medium-high heat. Add shallots and garlic; cook 4 to 5 minutes or until softened, stirring occasionally. Stir in mushrooms and marjoram. Cook 8 to 9 minutes or until all liquid has evaporated and the mushrooms begin to brown, stirring occasionally. Add sherry, salt and pepper; cook 1 minute.

3. Grease **CROCK-POT® LITTLE DIPPER®** slow cooker. Add mushroom mixture, crème fraîche and cheese. Cover; heat 1 hour. Stir well and serve with toasted baguette slices, flat bread or multi-grain crackers.

Makes about 1¼ cups

Variation: Try this dip served over steak or roast chicken.

Shrimp Fondue Dip

- **3 tablespoons butter, divided**
- **8 ounces small raw shrimp, peeled**
- **1 teaspoon seafood seasoning**
- **1/4 teaspoon black pepper**
- **1/4 teaspoon ground red pepper**
- **1 tablespoon all-purpose flour**
- **3/4 cup half-and-half**
- **3/8 cup (about 3 ounces) shredded Gruyère cheese**
- **1/4 cup dry white wine**
- **1 teaspoon Dijon mustard**
- **Sliced French bread**

1. Melt 2 tablespoons butter in medium saucepan over medium heat. Add shrimp and sprinkle with seafood seasoning, black pepper and red pepper. Cook 3 minutes or until shrimp are opaque, stirring frequently. Transfer to medium bowl.

2. Melt remaining 1 tablespoon butter in same saucepan over medium heat. Stir in flour; cook and stir 2 minutes. Gradually stir in half-and-half. Cook and stir until mixture comes to a boil and thickens. Add cheese; cook and stir until cheese is melted. Stir in wine, mustard and cooked shrimp with any accumulated juices.

3. Coat **CROCK-POT® LITTLE DIPPER®** slow cooker with nonstick cooking spray. Fill with warm dip. Serve with sliced French bread.

Makes about 1 3/4 cups

Barbecue Sloppy Joe Dip

- 2 teaspoons olive oil
- 12 ounces ground beef
- 1/3 cup finely chopped onion
- 1 clove garlic, minced
- 1/4 teaspoon dried oregano
- 1/4 cup barbecue sauce
- 2 tablespoons ketchup
- 2 teaspoons packed brown sugar
- 2 teaspoons cider vinegar
- 3/4 cup (about 3 ounces) shredded Monterey Jack cheese
- 1 tablespoon chopped fresh cilantro
- Sliced baguettes or tortilla chips

1. Brown beef in oil 6 to 8 minutes in large skillet over medium-high heat, stirring to break up meat. Stir in onion, garlic and oregano; cook 4 minutes. Remove from heat. Stir in barbecue sauce, ketchup, brown sugar and vinegar. Let cool 2 minutes; stir in cheese.

2. Transfer to **CROCK-POT® LITTLE DIPPER®** slow cooker. Cover; heat 1 hour or until cheese is melted. Stir well; sprinkle with cilantro. Serve with sliced baguettes or tortilla chips.

Makes about 1 1/2 cups

Pepperoni Pizza Dip

- 1 jar (about 14 ounces) pizza sauce
- 1/3 cup chopped turkey pepperoni
- 1/2 can (about 2 1/4 ounces) sliced black olives, drained
- 1 teaspoon dried oregano
- 1/4 cup (about 1 ounce) shredded mozzarella cheese
- 1/2 package (about 1 1/2 ounces) cream cheese, softened
- 1 tablespoon olive oil
- Breadsticks or pita chips

1. Combine pizza sauce, pepperoni, olives and oregano in medium saucepan. Bring to a boil over medium-high heat, stirring frequently. Reduce heat to low. Stir in mozzarella cheese and cream cheese. Cook and stir until melted. Remove from heat and stir in oil.

2. Coat **CROCK-POT® LITTLE DIPPER®** slow cooker with nonstick cooking spray. Fill with warm dip. Serve with breadsticks or pita chips.

Makes 1 1/3 cups

Spicy Korean Chicken Wings

2 tablespoons peanut oil, plus additional for frying
2 tablespoons grated ginger
1/2 cup reduced-sodium soy sauce
1/4 cup cider vinegar
1/4 cup honey
1/4 cup chili garlic sauce
2 tablespoons orange juice
1 tablespoon sesame oil
18 chicken wings or drummettes
Sesame seeds (optional)

1. Heat 2 tablespoons peanut oil in medium skillet over medium-high heat. Add ginger; cook and stir 2 minutes. Add soy sauce, vinegar, honey, chili garlic sauce, orange juice and sesame oil; cook and stir 2 minutes.

2. Heat 2 inches peanut oil in large heavy saucepan over medium-high heat until oil is 350° to 375°F.

3. Rinse chicken wings under cold water; pat dry with paper towels. Remove and discard wing tips. Add chicken wings to peanut oil and cook about 8 to 10 minutes or until crispy and brown and chicken is cooked through. Remove wings from peanut oil; drain on paper towels.

4. Add wings to sauce; toss to coat. Fill **CROCK-POT® LITTLE DIPPER®** slow cooker with as many wings as will fit. Reserve and keep warm any extra wings, refilling **CROCK-POT® LITTLE DIPPER®** slow cooker as space allows. Sprinkle with sesame seeds.

Makes 6 to 8 servings

Creamy Artichoke-Parmesan Dip

- **1 teaspoon olive oil**
- **2 tablespoons finely chopped onion**
- **1/2 can (about 7 ounces) artichoke hearts, drained and chopped**
- **1/2 cup half-and-half**
- **1/2 cup (about 2 ounces) mozzarella cheese**
- **1/3 cup mayonnaise**
- **1/3 grated Parmesan cheese**
- **1/8 teaspoon oregano**
- **1/8 teaspoon garlic powder**
- **4 pita bread rounds, toasted and cut into wedges**

1. Heat oil in medium saucepan over medium heat. Add onion; cook until translucent, stirring occasionally. Stir in remaining ingredients except pita wedges. Bring to a boil over medium heat, stirring frequently.

2. Coat **CROCK-POT® LITTLE DIPPER®** slow cooker with nonstick cooking spray. Fill with warm dip. Serve with pita wedges.

Makes 1 1/2 cups

Raspberry-Balsamic Glazed Meatballs

- **1 bag (2 pounds) frozen fully cooked meatballs**
- **1 cup raspberry preserves**
- **3 tablespoons sugar**
- **3 tablespoons balsamic vinegar**
- **1 tablespoon plus 1½ teaspoons Worcestershire sauce**
- **¼ teaspoon red pepper flakes**
- **1 tablespoon grated fresh ginger (optional)**

1. Coat **CROCK-POT®** slow cooker with nonstick cooking spray. Add frozen meatballs; set aside.

2. Combine preserves, sugar, vinegar, Worcestershire sauce and red pepper flakes in small microwavable bowl. Microwave on HIGH 45 seconds; stir. Microwave 15 seconds or until melted (mixture will be chunky). Reserve ½ cup mixture. Pour remaining mixture over meatballs; toss to coat well. Cover; cook on LOW 5 hours or on HIGH 2½ hours.

3. Turn **CROCK-POT®** slow cooker to HIGH. Stir in ginger, if desired, and reserved ½ cup preserve mixture. Cook, uncovered, 15 to 20 minutes or until thickened slightly, stirring occasionally.

Makes about 16 servings

Carmelized Onion Dip
(page 231)

Recipe Index

Recipe Index

Chicken Liver Pâté
(page 198)

Recipe Index

Recipe Index

Mexican Cheese Soup ***(page 31)***

Recipe Index

Peach Cobbler ***(page 167)***

Recipe Index

Braised Beets with Cranberries ***(page 109)***

Recipe Index

Warm Peanut-Caramel Dip *(page 236)*

Metric Chart

VOLUME MEASUREMENTS (dry)

1/8 teaspoon = 0.5 mL
1/4 teaspoon = 1 mL
1/2 teaspoon = 2 mL
3/4 teaspoon = 4 mL
1 teaspoon = 5 mL
1 tablespoon = 15 mL
2 tablespoons = 30 mL
1/4 cup = 60 mL
1/3 cup = 75 mL
1/2 cup = 125 mL
2/3 cup = 150 mL
3/4 cup = 175 mL
1 cup = 250 mL
2 cups = 1 pint = 500 mL
3 cups = 750 mL
4 cups = 1 quart = 1 L

VOLUME MEASUREMENTS (fluid)

1 fluid ounce (2 tablespoons) = 30 mL
4 fluid ounces (1/2 cup) = 125 mL
8 fluid ounces (1 cup) = 250 mL
12 fluid ounces (1 1/2 cups) = 375 mL
16 fluid ounces (2 cups) = 500 mL

WEIGHTS (mass)

1/2 ounce = 15 g
1 ounce = 30 g
3 ounces = 90 g
4 ounces = 120 g
8 ounces = 225 g
10 ounces = 285 g
12 ounces = 360 g
16 ounces = 1 pound = 450 g

DIMENSIONS

1/16 inch = 2 mm
1/8 inch = 3 mm
1/4 inch = 6 mm
1/2 inch = 1.5 cm
3/4 inch = 2 cm
1 inch = 2.5 cm

OVEN TEMPERATURES

250°F = 120°C
275°F = 140°C
300°F = 150°C
325°F = 160°C
350°F = 180°C
375°F = 190°C
400°F = 200°C
425°F = 220°C
450°F = 230°C

BAKING PAN AND DISH EQUIVALENTS

Utensil	Size in Inches	Size in Centimeters	Volume	Metric Volume
Baking or Cake Pan (square or rectangular)	8×8×2	20×20×5	8 cups	2 L
	9×9×2	23×23×5	10 cups	2.5 L
	13×9×2	33×23×5	12 cups	3 L
Loaf Pan	8½×4½×2½	21×11×6	6 cups	1.5 L
	9×9×3	23×13×7	8 cups	2 L
Round Layer Cake Pan	8×1½	20×4	4 cups	1 L
	9×1½	23×4	5 cups	1.25 L
Pie Plate	8×1½	20×4	4 cups	1 L
	9×1½	23×4	5 cups	1.25 L
Baking Dish or Casserole			1 quart/4 cups	1 L
			1½ quart/6 cups	1.5 L
			2 quart/8 cups	2 L
			3 quart/12 cups	3 L